Trading S&P Futures and Options

A Survival Manual and Study Guide

by

Humphrey E. D. Lloyd

TRADERS PRESS, INC.®

I N C O R P O R A T E D

P.O. BOX 6206
GREENVILLE, S.C. 29606

Books and Gifts
for Investors and Traders

Publishers of:

Commodity Spreads: A Historical Chart Perspective (Dobson)
The Trading Rule That Can Make You Rich* (Dobson)
Viewpoints of a Commodity Trader (Longstreet)
Commodities: A Chart Anthology (Dobson)
Profitable Grain Trading (Ainsworth)
A Complete Guide to Trading Profits (Paris)
Traders Guide to Technical Analysis (Hardy)
The Professional Commodity Trader (Kroll)
Jesse Livermore: Speculator-King (Sarnoff)
Understanding Fibonacci Numbers (Dobson)
Wall Street Ventures & Adventures through Forty Years (Wyckoff)
Winning Market Systems (Appel)
How to Trade in Stocks (Livermore)
Stock Market Trading Systems (Appel & Hitschler)
Study Helps in Point and Figure Technique (Wheelan)
Commodity Spreads: Analysis, Selection and Trading Techniques (Smith)
Comparison of Twelve Technical Trading Systems (Lukac, Brorsen, & Irwin)
Day Trading with Short Term Price Patterns and Opening Range Breakout (Crabel)
Understanding Bollinger Bands (Dobson)
Chart Reading for Professional Traders (Jenkins)
Geometry of Stock Market Profits (Jenkins)

Please write or call for our current catalog describing these and many other books and gifts of interest to investors and traders.

1-800-927-8222   FAX 864-298-0221
Tradersprs@aol.com

This picture was taken on Tuesday morning April 16, 1996. Jump-master Bob from Surrey England, photographer Ian and Humphrey from Beverly, MA are at 7000 feet--give or take a few feet-- traveling at 120 mph-- terminal velocity. We are over the Island of *Providenciales* (Provo) in the Turks and Caicos group of islands.

Just as Bob got me down on target safely, so it is my hope that I can guide you, be your jump-master if you like, so that you can learn to play this exciting game without significant financial injury.

Dedication

This Book Is Dedicated To
David Edward Lloyd

May the selection and money management skills
you demonstrate in Las Vegas travel with your orders
over the telephone lines to Chicago.

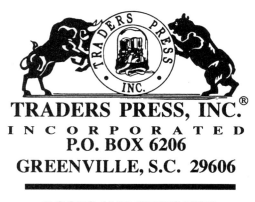

TRADERS PRESS, INC.®
I N C O R P O R A T E D
P.O. BOX 6206
GREENVILLE, S.C. 29606

BOOKS AND GIFTS FOR
TRADERS AND INVESTORS

TRADERS PRESS, INC. stocks hundreds of titles of interest to investors and traders in stocks, options, and futures. In addition, we carry a full line of gift items for investors. Please contact us, and we will gladly forward you our current *"TRADER'S CATALOG"* by return mail.

800-927-8222   Fax 864-298-0221
Tradersprs@aol.com
http://traderspress.com

IMPORTANT ADVICE

From a Declaration of Principles jointly adopted by a Committee of the American Bar Association and a Committee of Publishers.

Hamlet: William Shakespeare.

Acknowledgments

The MetaStock™ charts in this publication are used by permission of
Equis International, Inc.,
3950 South 700 East, Suite 100, Salt Lake City, UT 84107
1-800-882-3040 or 801-265-8886,
Fax 801-265-3999.

http://www.equis.com.

Nearly all the charts in this manual have been generated by MetaStock™. Thanks also
to North Systems, 6821 Lemongrass Loop SE, Salem, Oregon 97306, 503-364-3829, Fax
503-391-5929, E-Mail NorthSys@aol.com for permission to use charts from CandlePower™4.

Also, special thanks to my good friends Matthew N. Xiarhos who helped me become computer
friendly and Vilar F. Kelly for the gift of *Trophy*.

TABLE OF CONTENTS

INTRODUCTION

The idea for this manual came to me in the 'T and M' zone — *the thought and meditation zone* — it occurs around 5 a.m., often a little beforehand, when it's too early to get up and too late to try to get back to sleep.

As background I have been -- indeed still am -- a successful stock market and mutual fund investor. I have made some significant money for myself and for a few friends whose accounts I handled from 1982 through 1992. So anyone who can make a bundle in the stock market should have no trouble trading the S&P futures market. A piece of cake, right? Wrong, and for several reasons. This manual will give details concerning the ways that things can go awry and the pitfalls to avoid. Since the mistakes I made cost me about $15,000, I think I know something about them. As Edwin Lefevre said in *Reminiscences of a Stock Operator* [2], "The mistake family is so large that there is always one of them around when you want to see what you can do in the fool-play line." Also, "All stock market mistakes wound you in two tender spots -- your pocketbook and your vanity."

Since I am not claiming any primary expertise in making money in the futures or options markets, I do not feel I have to document my trading losses. They exist, indeed they do. This manual is for David and other intelligent newcomers to the S&P markets to show them how easy it is to go wrong; also to give some trading suggestions with charts and patterns to study. My mistakes cost me more than I had anticipated. Hopefully, exposing them to honest and dispassionate analysis may -- will -- should -- make the avoidance of similar mistakes a good deal easier for new futures traders.

It helps to look on trading as a game, a game with a number of similarities to the game of golf. And every golfer knows the key to a good score is to keep the ball in play. So with the analogy of golf in mind, several aspects of the trading game will be examined with the idea of avoiding mistakes and keeping the ball in play.

Before we go any further, I should explain how this manual has been set up. All the text is on the right-hand page and the various aspects of the trading game are considered in what I hope will be a logical sequence. Where charts or diagrams are necessary to explain comments in the text, such charts will be on the opposing left-hand page. However, there is also a study guide using, for the most part, six-minute charts set up with an indicator, plus a candlestick chart with Bollinger Bands based on a 13-bar moving average and a single point (SP) chart with a 7 bar triangular moving average (for Triangular MA's see pg. 55). Don't worry about any of the details now. All will be explained in the text. Charts for the month of May 1996 form the basis of the study guide with selected additional charts chosen to illustrate important market concepts. These charts will appear on the left-hand pages.

Notes on the Charts

May was a great trading month, so **please** do not expect results from **Angler, Embryo** and **Ravine** to be as successful, in an average month, as they were in May `96. May was chosen for no other reason than that it was the month dead ahead of my writing. The reader can analyze the trading patterns and confirm their performance. An important point I want to make, and it is important, is that these patterns were in no way optimized for the month of May. These are the patterns I have isolated by my own observations over many months of trading. There will be times they work very well and other times when they clearly do not.

The charts themselves are in a way unique as I have juxtaposed candlestick and single point (SP or close only) charts, the latter beneath the former so that they may be compared; in effect providing a "toggle" between them.

THE STUDY GUIDE

I SUGGEST YOU READ THE TEXT IN ITS ENTIRETY BEFORE PAYING SERIOUS ATTENTION TO THE STUDY GUIDE.

Deciding Which Course To Play

Just as there are courses that range from a putting layout -- a pitch and putt course -- a par 3 course -- a short easy course to a long and fiendishly difficult course like Pebble Beach, so there are many layouts to play in the S&P futures and options markets. I believe the decision about which course to play is one of the most important ones confronting the S&P trader and the most difficult one to make.

What are the possibilities? They range from day trading using 3 or even 1 minute bars, all the way through to long term position trading involving holding a position for many weeks or even months.

The Basics

The shorter the time frame, the smaller the profit is likely to be. But the trade-off is that profits will be quicker, and hopefully occur more frequently and stops can be smaller. Options offer a way of reducing volatility.

What To Expect

A difficult running-in period as a personal trading style and approach has to be found. I believe it is only by developing one's personal style -- system if you like -- that long-term success can be achieved. That is not to say that it **will** be achieved, only that one has to develop one's own "swing." Though all good golfers perform certain key moves as they swing through the ball, the way they do so is highly individualistic. Even at 100 paces Lee Trevino's swing is instantly recognizable and distinguishable, without possibility of confusion, from that of Arnold Palmer. This running-in period is what cost me most of my tuition money. Though I have started with a discussion of deciding on which course to play, actually this decision should be made only after we have examined the other aspects of the game.

Mistakes To Avoid

The worst mistake is jumping around from system to system, course to course, approach to approach. Paper trading is often suggested as a way of finding one's own style without cost. Paper trading is like miniature golf — it has no relation to the real thing and it does not work because no money is on the line.

May 31, 1996

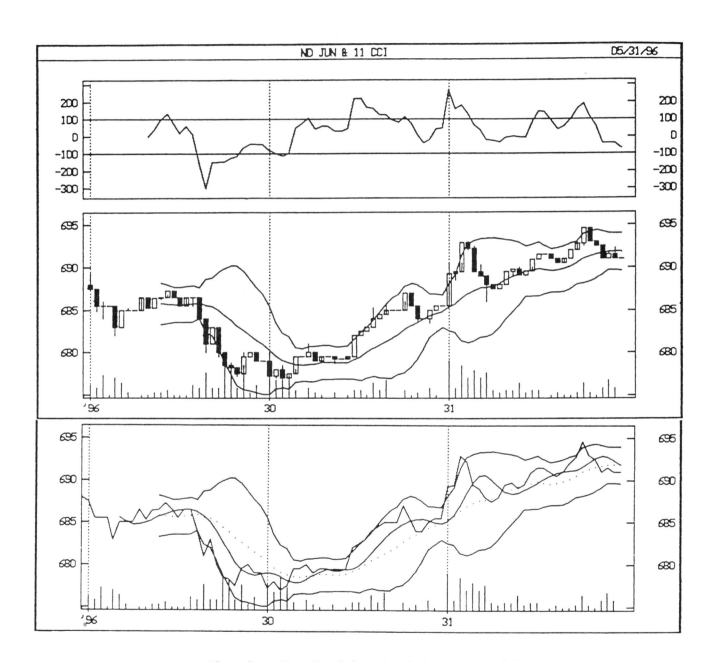

Chart from MetaStock from Equis International, Inc.

This is a chart of the **Jun NASDAQ** contract for 5/31/96. As you see, the trading is thin. The time frame is 15 minutes per bar.

Trading Suggestion

Find a trading buddy and call in your trades exactly as you would to your broker. **More than anything else one needs practice at picking up the phone and calling the order in.** Decide on the multiplier. The S&P futures trade at 500 times their stated value, so a move of one dollar in the futures contract means a gain or loss of 500 dollars. It is the size of this multiplier that is one of the main reasons S&P trading is so difficult (but also very profitable if successful). You are playing at the $500 tables unless, that is, you take my trading suggestion and use a multiplier with your buddy of, say 50 instead of 500, and learn to play at lesser cost. Note the minimum change (1 tick) allowed in the S&P futures contract value is 5 cents (5 points). At x 500 this represents $25. A move in the futures of one dollar is 100 points. Unfortunately, this is sometimes referred to as **one** point in line with a move on the DJIA -- the Dow. So be forewarned.

Here is another **trading suggestion**. Recently (April 1996) futures and options trading began on the *Chicago Mercantile Exchange* (CME) on the **NASDAQ** 100 index. The multiplier is **100**. Presently the contract is thinly traded but this should improve. I think it would pay to look into trading NASDAQ futures and options as a way of learning to trade at less risk.

Here's what I suggest when using the buddy approach. Keep proper records, and if your buddy isn't home when you put your trade in, put the trade on an answering machine. It is essential to get into the habit of picking up the phone and making a commitment to the trade. At the end of the week, work out who has won, who has lost, **and pay up**. Some money **must** be riding. You can even play with your spouse as long as you get the order and time phoned on record. In this way any gains/losses stay within the family. This trading suggestion may not only save you alot of money, but convince you that S&P trading is not for you, which may save you more money and a good deal of frustration. But, of course, the rewards -- which can be very substantial -- will not be there either.

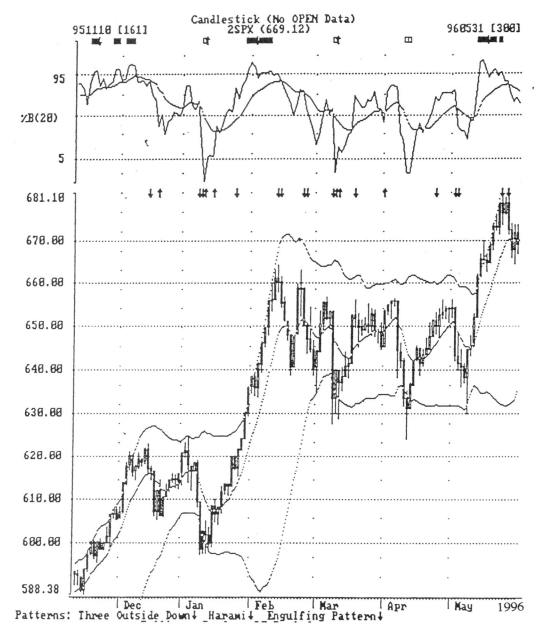

Candlestick (No OPEN Data)
2SPX (669.12)

951110 [161]   960531 [300]

%B shows market position relative to the Bollinger Bands

Notice how 'to and through' bands carri through to the upsid during this time peri but not to the down side.

Patterns: Three Outside Down↓ Harami↓ Engulfing Pattern↓

Chart from **North Systems CandlePower**™4 Chart of S&P Cash Index to give **the big picture.** (No opening gaps are shown.)

*Gary works out the present futures price from the Cash Index and the futures premium to cash as these values go by on the tape.

Selecting The Correct Equipment

The Basics

If you are going to trade within the day -- "day trade" -- you have two choices.

1) **Use a 'Set-It and Forget-It' system**. There are only a few good ones out there. Vilar Kelly's *Trophy*[3] is one of the best I know (his *Daycare* system is highly rated also). For *Trophy* you enter open high low and close figures for the current S&P contract at the end of the day, and you add the next day's opening price as soon as it is known. The program will then generate a complete set of instructions for the trading day. *Daycare* parameters are easily calculated the night before as the new opening price is not used. Both systems have winning track records.

Indeed, *Trophy* had a trade recently that took $2800 per contract out of the market in a most instructive fashion. The system went to a $2200 or so profit before backing off. Most screen watchers would, I suspect, have taken $1000 or so profit and exited the trade, but the system said to stay in the trade. The market then moved back in the original direction to log the great profit recorded above.

The set-it, forget-it — give the orders to the broker — let's play golf approach — has a great deal to be said for it. No expensive quote service is needed. No time need be spent in front of the computer screen and a good chance of profit, on an ongoing basis, exists. So what are the drawbacks? Well, there is no ego satisfaction for a start. Some other player is hitting the ball for you. There is also that uncertainty until the results are in at the end of the day... well, did I make some money or didn't I? Also, for some reason, losses seem tougher to take with such systems. However, for certain people I suspect that playing the S&P in this fashion is the best way to go. Recently I came across another such system that looks very promising programmed by William B. Brower.[4] He calls it *SP Season Daytrade*.

2) **Get a live, real-time quote service.** If your name is Gary Smith[5] or you trade the way he does, all you will need is the *CNBC* news service with its continuous updates.* My mind is not attunedto this kind of data processing, so I use Signal[6] with MetaStock™[7] version 4.52 RT. I like this combination very much, though, of course, there are others out there. This set up will run you close to $3000 a year which includes exchange fees, levied by the Chicago Mercantile Exchange (CME), so you are down each year by that amount before you start trading.

SPM 96

This is a copy of my own Candlestick chart of the S&P Jun (SPM) Futures. Note the big opening gap on Apr 8 and the length of time it took to get filled. See comment on pg. 53 about getting a feel for the market.

What To Expect

Things will go wrong and just at the wrong time. The dog will dive under the desk and pull the plug on your receiver or the electricity will be shut off for some reason or there will be transmission of data problems (though fortunately very rarely).

Mistakes To Avoid

When the market is really running either up or down, even "real time" data may be delayed by many seconds; sometimes, though rarely, by a minute or more. Under these circumstances, it is essential to know what the broker shows on his screen, otherwise slippage may be unacceptable. I have trained myself **always** to ask, "What does your screen show for the S&P?" before putting an order in. Another mistake to avoid relates to tick data. Although this is rare, your screen may not show the market has traded at a particular tick---to repeat a tick is 5 points (5 cents worth $25) when in fact it did trade there for a second or so. If you had a stop order at that very tick, and it has happened to me on more than one occasion, you may find yourself stopped into or out of a trade without realizing it. This can really cost and you have to bear the expense of somebody else's error.

So I have learned to push my broker for an order check if I see a tick recorded one tick away from my signal tick. There will be more on this problem under orders.

If you are not going to day-trade but position trade instead, you will still need reliable data. *CNBC* plus the *Wall Street Journal* (WSJ) and/or *Investors Business Daily* (IBD) should be fine. If you decide to trade options, you will definitely need *IBD* as the option tables are more extensive than the *Journal's*.

It is, of course, obvious that equipment selection will vary with the type of trading selected. Here is another **trading suggestion**. See if you can locate a neighbor with a real-time quote service and ask if you can spend a day or two observing the screen. If you sit down in front of the screen about 9:25 EST to catch the opening of the S&P in Chicago at 8:30 Central Time, you may find that by 11 am EST you feel mentally fatigued and rather bored, yet you still have 5 hours trading left to run! This may cure you of wanting to trade full time. Of course, there may well be other reasons for wanting to do so. I am retired now but I had always wanted to trade for a living. I thank my lucky stars that I did not retire early to do so as I would not have been able to support my family properly by trading. Having a regular job is much easier, believe me, unless you can trade like Larry Williams [8] with big stops and a debonair approach.

Now we will run all the daily charts for May 96. They will be in order, but the sequence will be interrupted when comments made on the right hand page need clarification and/or illustration.

The figures directly under the chart are:

OPEN   HIGH   LOW   CLOSE

The figure next to Angler is the *'bait point'* and the arrow denotes the short term trend. Finally, any special points are noted under comment.

Understanding Candlesticks

The **real body** of the candle is formed by the opening value and the value at the close of the bar. If the close is higher than the open, a white candle is formed. If the close is lower than the open, a black candle is formed. The high and low of the bar form the **shadows**.

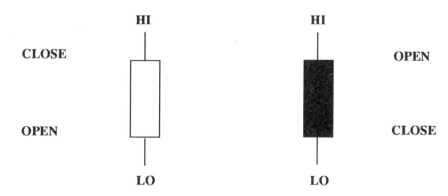

If you cannot find a neighbor with a quote screen, see if you can find a broker who will let you watch a live screen of the S&P. Some brokers have screens for the use of their customers, but you will have to share time with those other customers so the friendly neighbor is the better bet.

There is also one other way of trying to take profits from S&P futures and options, and that is to decide exactly how you wish to trade and exactly what signals you wish to use and then find a broker who will monitor the market for you constantly during the day and trade for you. You will have to make the original decisions and in order to do so you will be helped by this text and the study guide. (See final trading suggestion #5 on pg. 129)

May 1, 1996

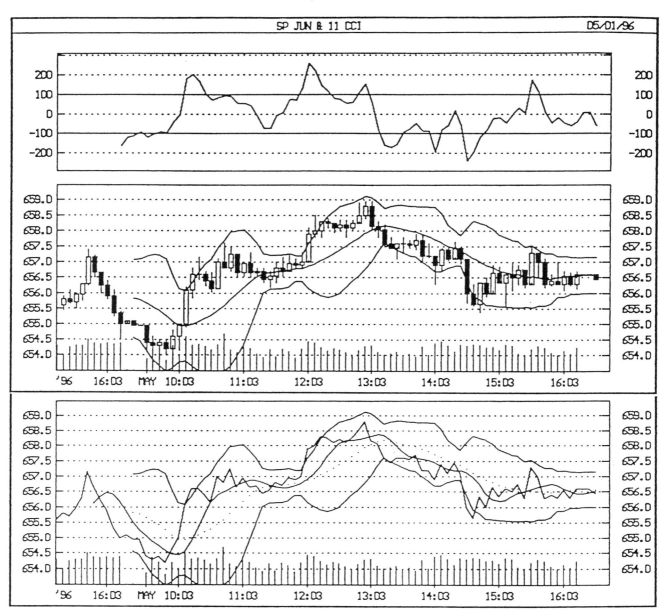

	654.50		658.95		654.00		656.45
							P/L
Angler: ↑ 654.50	B	654.50	S	656.35	+1.85		
Embryo:	B	656.30	S	657.55	+1.25		

Ravine: No Trade (NT)

Comment: Notice negative divergence on CCI 11 around 13:03. Profit/Loss (P/L) figures are given in **dollars** (not points).

Selecting A Broker

The Basics

A broker is an order-taker, period. And the less you spend on commissions, the better your bottom line will be. Do not ask anyone for advice --- and that includes your broker. You have to form your own opinion of the market and get the orders in accurately. You have a responsibility to give the orders clearly and unambiguously to your broker, and the broker's responsibility is to repeat them to you and execute them.

So, should you go with a discount broker? Well, the answer is partly in the form of a statement - what you do **not** want to do is go with a full-service "name" broker at a stock market house with a commodity department. You will be charged around $90 round-turn (commodities, unlike stocks, are traded on round turn commissions; i.e., you pay a single fee --- just one --- to get in and get out).

I have found the deep discount brokers, whose typical charge of $15-20 a round turn per contract, while fine, leave something to be desired in the order execution department. What to look for is an experienced outfit with charges of no more than $25 per round turn. (There will be small National Futures Association and exchange fee charges in addition.) **Trading suggestion**: join *Club 3000*[9] and ask for members' experiences. *Club 3000* has an active membership. Articles and reviews are submitted by members and the biweekly publication will, I know, prove to be of real value to newcomers to commodity trading.

What To Expect

A clean clear-cut relationship. You give the orders, the broker executes them. Individual trades should be confirmed promptly-first by telephone, then by confirmation slip. Monthly statements should be sent in a timely manner, plus a calendar of upcoming important reports (pg. 67) plus option expiration dates, etc.

Mistakes To Avoid

The biggest mistakes to avoid involve sloppy order giving and record-keeping. If you say 'buy' but mean 'sell,' you are not going to go far in this game. There will be some suggestions later for avoiding such a mistake. For now, I suggest that you call your broker to check your position and net liquidating value any day you have an open position or have had a day-trade the previous day. In this way, mistakes, either yours or theirs, can be picked up without delay. It is best to call before trading starts.

Buy Stop

This is placed *above* the market. You wish to enter or exit the market if it reaches point **B**.

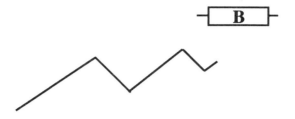

Sell Stop

This is placed *below* the market. You wish to enter or exit the market if it reaches point **S**.

Limit-OB (or better)

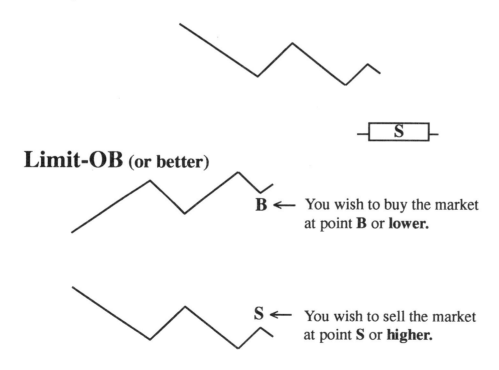

B ← You wish to buy the market at point **B** or **lower.**

S ← You wish to sell the market at point **S** or **higher.**

Types of Orders

The Basics

The commonly used orders are:

a) At The Market - ATM

This means I want in/out **now** at the best possible price.

b) A Buy Stop

This is placed **above** the market and is used to enter a long (buy) position. In this case the position is entered on strength. This order is also used to exit a short (sell) position.

c) A Sell Stop

This is placed **below** the market and is used to enter the market on weakness or exit a long (buy) position.

d) A Limit Order

A buy order is to enter/exit the market at a specified price or lower. It is placed **at or below** the market. A sell order is to enter/exit the market at a specified price or higher. It is placed **at or above** the market.

e) Market-If-Touched - MIT

This becomes a market order as soon as the specified price is reached.

f) Market On Close - MOC

An order to buy or sell in the closing range.

g) Order Cancels Order - OCO

One order executed cancels the other order on the books.

h) Fill Or Kill - FOK

An order to be filled immediately at a specified price. If nothing done, order is killed.

i) Contingent Order

If an order is filled, then an order contingent on the fill is activated on a not-held basis (not held responsible if impossible to execute).

What To Expect & Mistakes To Avoid

At The Market

If the market is running your actual fill may be far from where you expect. This is known as **slippage**. It is better to avoid market orders altogether for entry. Certainly it is a mistake to do so in a fast market. If you are long the market, you can use market orders to exit if the market is moving in your direction. Under these circumstances, you may get positive slippage when you sell receiving more than expected.

May 2, 1996

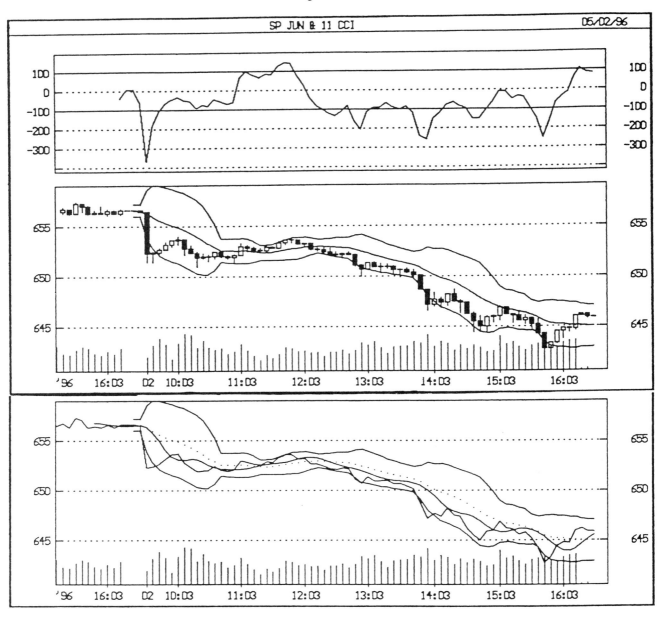

| 651.45 | 654.00 | 642.20 | 645.85 |

Angler:	↑ 655.65	NT	P/L	
Embryo:	B 653.25	S 652.00	-1.25	} +0.60
	S 649.65	B 647.80	+1.85	
Ravine:	S 651.40	B 647.85	+3.65	

Comments: This is a downside runner with almost a 1200 point range.

I seldom use market orders and never do so if I am going to stop and reverse (SAR). If I have bought the market and am proved wrong, I need to get out (sell) on a stop and then reverse (sell an additional contract) if the market gives me a reason for doing so. If I stop and reverse 'at the market,' I run the risk of slippage on both sell positions-the one that terminates the buy trade and the one that initiates the sell trade.

Stop Orders

Slippage can and will occur on stop orders as these orders become market orders as soon as the stop price is hit. A way to avoid slippage is to give a **stop with limit order.** Say you want to buy the S&P if the price reaches 650. You can give the order as buy 1 Jun S&P contract at 650 **stop** 650.10 **limit.** This means you will accept 2 ticks slippage but not more. If you say 650 **stop limit,** you are saying you do not want to be filled at any price higher than your stop price. The danger here is not getting filled at all, as the market moves into and past your stop.

Limit Orders

Here it pays not to get too cute. Let's say the S&P is trading at 650 again and you want to buy it. You can enter a limit order to buy it at 650 or better, or at any price you elect below 650. Let's say you decide the market will back down to 649.50 before resuming its advance. If you enter an order to buy 1 Jun S&P contract at 649.50 **OB-or better** (which means or **lower** on the buy side), you run a very definite risk of not getting filled as the market has to trade at 649.45 for you to be sure you are filled. Just touching 649.50 momentarily does not guarantee a fill. It is a mistake therefore to enter a limit order away from the market by more than a few ticks, particularly if you miss a really good trade by doing so.

Market If Touched

Since this order becomes a market order as soon as the specified market price is touched, slippage again may occur, in fact usually does. But you will get in or out somewhere near your price.

May 3, 1996

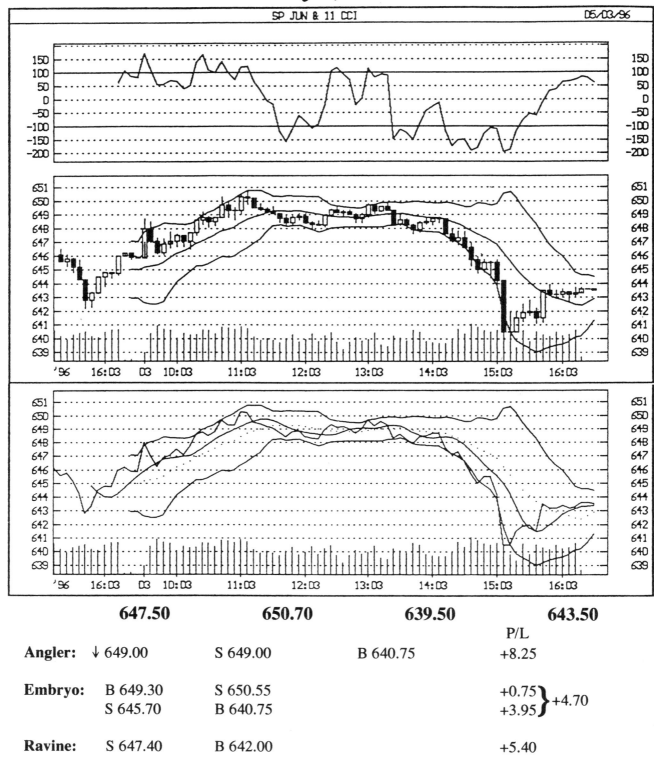

	647.50	650.70	639.50	643.50
				P/L
Angler:	↓ 649.00	S 649.00	B 640.75	+8.25
Embryo:	B 649.30	S 650.55		+0.75 ⎫
	S 645.70	B 640.75		+3.95 ⎭ +4.70
Ravine:	S 647.40	B 642.00		+5.40

Comment: This is a classic pivot day with a great **Ravine** formation.

Market On Close

Gary Smith often uses this order to exit a day trade. He believes in staying with a profitable trade to the very end, particularly as the floor can run the trade up considerably in the last 15 minutes from 4:00 PM EST when the cash S&P market closes to 4:15 when the futures market closes. I have never been fond of this order. Also I believe that it is a mistake to use it when trading options, as you can nearly always get a better price before the closing range.

Order Cancels Order

This is a cumbersome way to trade and better avoided. The same goes for fill or kill.

Contingent Order

This order is useful if one has to be away from the screen. I have used it in connection with option trading, but I am uncomfortable trading away from the screen and so seldom use it. There are two other orders I should mention.

Straight Cancel

This order is self explanatory.

Cancel - Replace

This order is used for moving stops---trailing stops---closer to the market. Once a stop is in, do not lower a sell stop or raise a buy stop to "give the market more room." It is usually a costly mistake to do so and certainly an action to be avoided. Use the cancel-replace order to raise sell stops (protecting more profit) or lower buy stops as the market trends lower.

GIVING ORDERS

The Basics

We have covered the different types of orders, now they need to be transmitted clearly and precisely.

Trading Recommendation

Use the **trading order form** I have designed or design your own but use one. Decide what you want to do---also, know what you will do if proved wrong.

Now **write it down**. Then read it to your broker. The order goes like this: "Hi, this is Dave Lloyd A/C #12345. I wish to **buy**--- that is **buy**---one Jun S&P at 650 even **on a stop**."

TRADING ORDER FORM

DATE 4-22-96				**DAY** MON		
A-C# 12345				**Tel #** 1-800-978-4554		
BUY	(B)					
SELL		(S)				
# MONTH	1 JUN	1 JUN				
STOP AT	650	648.75				
LIMIT OB						
ATM						
MIT						
TICKET #	543	548				
AGENT	CHUCK	CHRIS				
TIME	10:22	10:25				
CANCEL						
C/REPLACE						
TICKET #						
TIME						

The Jun S&P contract is **SPM.**

Note: Since Jun is the next contract to expire, your broker will assume you wish to trade this contract if you do not mention the month.

Note: You do not need to say it is a **day order**---that is assumed unless you specify that it is an **open** order (good till canceled or GTC). I usually repeat 'buy' to be sure of getting it right. The broker will repeat the order back to you and give you a ticket number. Enter the name of the person taking the order and the time the order was entered on the trading order form.

What To Expect

Your entry stop is hit. Note the time you saw it on the screen. Now call back and place a **sell stop once you are sure you have been filled**. This is a **protective stop**. It can be placed at the same time that you place your original order. I prefer to call back soon after my entry point is hit. This gives me a chance to ask about my fill. It is a matter of personal preference so **Golden Rule #1:** *Use a protective stop for all futures trades.* (Stops cannot be placed on spread orders with options.) You will have been filled when the market hits your stop provided your order was on the floor. It is a mistake to believe you have entered the market and bought (or sold) a contract if the time be tween calling your order in and seeing the print on the screen is short. You have to allow as much as 90 seconds to get the order working and, if things are very hectic, more.

Note: If you go "at the market," unless the action is very hot and heavy, most brokers will provide flash fills so you will know then and there---it only takes 30 seconds or so---what your exact price is.

Your sell stop is placed under the market. Here is the order. "Hi, this is Dave A/C # 12345. I wish to **sell**---that is **sell**---one Jun S&P at 648.75 **on a stop**." The broker repeats the order back to you and gives you a second ticket number. Note name, number and time on the order form. Now comes the sitting part.

Once you have your sell stop in, you have defined your trade. So why not walk away for half an hour or so and see what has happened when you return?

Indeed, why not? Well, human nature being what it is---or maybe it's just my nature being what it is---I find that very difficult to do. Indeed, I would, I'm sure, be a lot more successful if I could. But let's say you can do it, just walk away, say for 45 minutes, and what does the screen show on return to it?

Caramba! The market is trading at 651.65. Wow, you have 1.65 profit assuming you got filled at your price. That's $825. A mistake right there---that's called thinking about the money (I have never found a way to avoid it however). So, now what?

TRADING ORDER FORM

DATE 4-22-96			**DAY** MON			
A-C# 12345			**Tel #** 1-800-978-4554			
BUY	Ⓑ					
SELL		Ⓢ	Ⓢ			
# MONTH	1 JUN	1 JUN	1 JUN			
STOP AT	650.0	648.75	651.0			
LIMIT OB						
ATM						
MIT						
TICKET #	543	548				
AGENT	CHUCK	CHRIS	CHUCK			
TIME	10:22	10:25				
CANCEL						
C/REPLACE			548			
TICKET #			548-A			
TIME			11:10			

NB. Remember to straight cancel ticket 548-A if you EXIT-SELL on a profit objective.

Well, here is **Golden Rule #2**: *Never give back all the potential profit.* So you call up again and say, "Hi, this is Dave A/C # 12345. I wish to cancel and replace ticket # — give the sell ticket # — to sell one Jun S&P at 648.75 and **move the sell stop** to 651 even." The broker will repeat the order back to you and give you a new ticket # (usually the old one plus an "a"). Again note name, time and ticket #. Now you know you have a profit. The question is how much of a profit you will achieve. I tend to take the money soon and run, but that's not the most successful way. Here are your choices.

1) You can sell at a predetermined profit, say at 652.00 OB that gets $1000 minus commissions. **Remember to cancel the 651 sell stop.**

2) You can sell via a trailing stop — say at 150 points ($1.50) off the highest high of the day.

3) You can sell at a price MIT.

4) You can sell MOC.

Let's say the market runs to the close, a lucky day and one to be enjoyed, and you exit MOC with 280 points profit. Nice going. To achieve that profit you risked 125 points (your sell stop was at 648.75). There will be days inevitably when the market takes that from you slick as a whistle.

Mistakes To Avoid

Putting your stops too close--more of this later.

Not putting stops in at all--this one can kill you. Even Larry Williams uses stops of some sort. They may be 550 points away from entry, but they are stops nonetheless.

Trying to cancel or cancel/replace an order when the market is close to your price. You may think you have canceled but actually were too late. One good thing, they will usually call back pretty quickly on this one, but any delay can be costly.

Not allowing your profits to run---known as grabbing a small profit. This is a difficult mistake to avoid. Indeed, I wish I knew how to avoid it consistently. Probably the easiest mistake to make is just not getting the order in as a stop because you were going to do better as a limit order, and then to have the market crash through the stop you should have placed, and never look back. This is an opportunity lost and is costly, not in actual money but in potential gain. Also, such a mistake really tries the soul. You had it in your hand but didn't shut it fast enough. End result: no gain. It happened to me repeatedly until I forced myself to use stop orders for entry. Even the most torpid markets can spring suddenly to life and leave you standing in their dust. And it is really difficult to force oneself into a strong move once it is well under way.

OPTION SPREAD ORDER FORM

DATE ___2-21-96___   DAY ___WED___
AC# ___12345___   TEL# 1-800-978-4554

This is an S&P Option Spread Order

To open ___✓___   DAY ORDER ___✓___
To close _____   OPEN ORDER_____

I wish to

BUY	SELL
#_____1_____	#_____1_____
MONTH MAR	MONTH MAR
STRIKE 645	STRIKE 655
TYPE CALL	TYPE CALL

For a premium of ___450___ OB

To the ___BUY SIDE MAR 645 CALL___

TICKET# ___482___
AGENT ___STEVE___
TIME ___10:32___

Special Problems with Option Orders

The Basics

The basics are the same as for regular futures orders.

What To Expect

Floor traders will take every advantage of you they can. Option quotes are updated less frequently than futures quotes, and your fills for 'at the market' orders may be atrocious.

Mistakes To Avoid

Giving market orders. A good option broker can save you a considerable amount of money, most of the time, if you let him/her decide when to execute the order. This is known as **disregard tape** (DRT). It can get hairy at times if you are looking to get out of a position. If you really need to get out, you may have no choice but to go at the market. For entry it is a mistake to use market orders. It is far better to decide on the price you want to pay (or need to receive if selling options) and go with limit orders.

Spread orders where one option is bought and another sold should be given in terms of the basis, either as a debit of x number of points or less if the option bought costs more than the option sold or as a credit if more is received for the option sold than paid for the one bought. Here is a simple bull debit spread order. Use the option order form. "Hi, this is Dave A/C # 12345. This is an S&P **option spread order** good for today only. I wish to **buy** 1 MAR 645 S&P call and to **sell** 1 MAR 655 S&P call for a premium of 450 points **or less** to the buy side MAR 645 call." Note, you are not concerned with the actual purchase and sale prices of the two options, only that you do not pay more, are debited more than 450 points for putting on the spread. Options are a legitimate way to play the game. The options course has its own obstacles which we will have to examine further when we return to deciding on which course to play.

Also, avoid **good till canceled (GTC or open)** orders unless you are prepared to review them everyday. The danger, of course, is forgetting about the order only to find it has been executed when the position is no longer attractive.

May 6, 1996

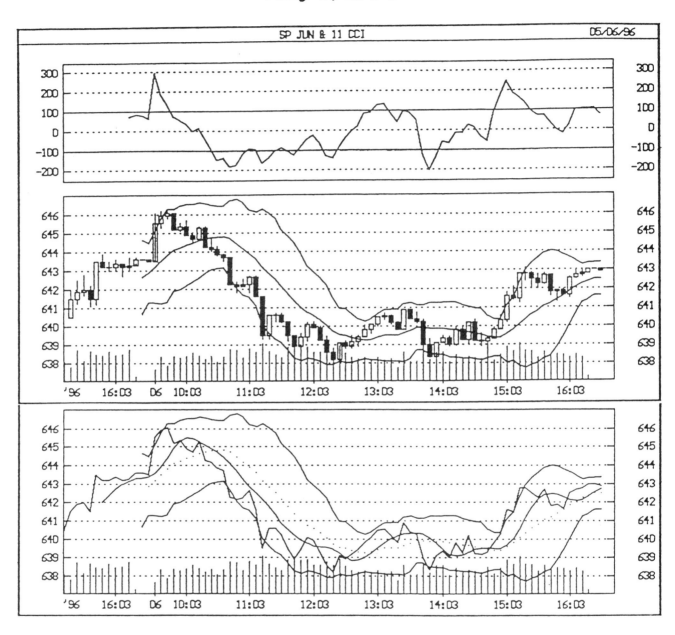

646.00	646.20	637.90	642.90
			P/L

Angler: ↓ 646.50   NT

Embryo: S 644.20   B 640.55   +3.65

Ravine: NT

Comment: Basically, a pivot day. Notice RP's in morning down move. (pg. 50)

Record-keeping

The Basics

If you use the **trading order form**, record-keeping should be a snap. All the pertinent data will be on the form. This form should then be filed with the confirmation slip for the trade when this is received. After a day trade, remember to check that you are flat the market. Also, tell your broker what you reckon your **net liquidating value** (Net Lik) should be. This is easily calculated from the net profit/loss from the trade plus the commission cost applied to the previous net liquidating value. This value is what the **cash portion of your account is worth**. It does not include any T-Bills you may own. The total account value is the net liquidating value plus the present value of any T-Bills.

What To Expect

Mistakes will be made. You exited a trade going flat the market but a keypunch error on their part still has you long or short the market in an overnight position. This, of course, completely invalidates the net liquidating value. The house will pick up on its mistake but you can speed things up by pointing out the error immediately. Hopefully the error will not be yours, such as would occur for instance if you were long and you said 'buy' when you meant 'sell' to close the position. This mistake will get you long 2 contracts and could be very costly if the market took a big hit. If you made this mistake and the market advanced, your account would be noticeably enriched but certainly not by any skill, just dumb luck. This mistake has not happened to me because I repeat the buy or sell command and because I have everything written out on the trading order form before I call the order in. Also, I listen carefully when the broker repeats my order, so hopefully it won't happen to me, but if it does I would be surprised if the mistake went in my favor.

Mistakes To Avoid

Failing to keep your trading order form to check against the confirmation slip. I keep all the slips until the monthly statement has been received. If everything checks out, I then dispose of the individual trading slips. Monthly statements are kept for at least three years. Another mistake to avoid is that of tying up too much of your cash in T-Bills. Your broker may allow you to use T-Bills at a high percentage of margin — the good faith money you need to have in the account to trade. If you have a $21,000 a/c it is a mistake to buy a $20,000 T-Bill as that really does not leave enough free cash---net liquidating value---in the account when the market, as it will, goes against you. T-Bills are purchased at discount to face value and mature in multiples of three months. If you need more cash in the account, you will have to cash in the T-Bill and that will cost you about $50 as will the original purchase. So you want to avoid this mistake and buy a $15,000 T-Bill instead.

May 7, 1996

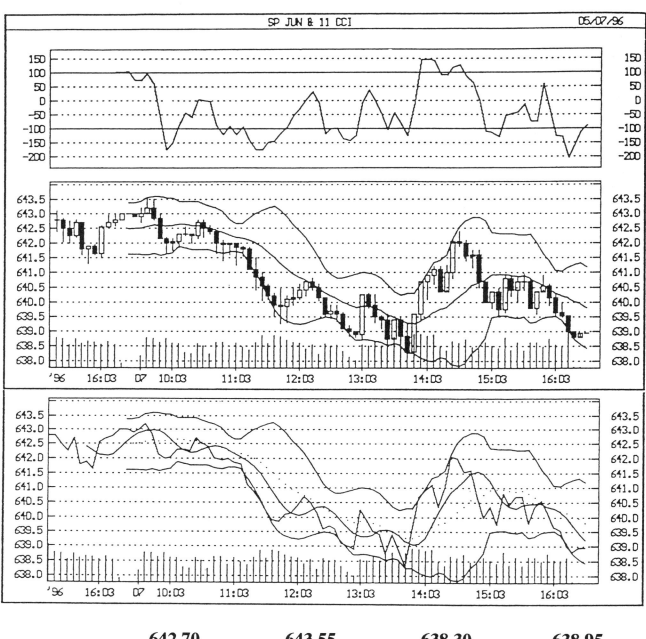

	642.70	643.55	638.30	638.95
				P/L
Angler:	↓ 645.25	NT		
Embryo:	S 640.90	B 639.70		+1.00
Ravine:	NT			

Comment: W formation around 13.30 followed by RP takeout on upper band. Good for 100 points. Good second time through +100 sell on CCI around 14.30.

Note: Margin in the commodities market differs fundamentally from margin in the stock market. In the latter, margin is just money borrowed from your broker. You share ownership of the stock which he carries on his books in street name — the name of the house — not in your name. You bear all the risk, of course. If your share — because of adverse market action — gets too low, you will get a margin call to ante up more money or your position will be sold out forthwith. In the commodities market, margin represents the amount of money-in cash and T-Bills-that you have to have in the account to trade commodities. Margin requirements vary. Presently an over-night position in the S&P futures requires $15,120 in margin. Such a sum of money assures the broker that you can settle your debts. No ownership is involved.

I believe it is essential to keep a trading diary. If you have a live quote system, I suggest you print up the chart of the action of a day you took a trade or trades and mark your entry and exit points in the day's chart. This exercise will help in the identification of mistakes and the human tendency to repeat them. It will also draw your attention to the amount of money left on the table.

May 8, 1996

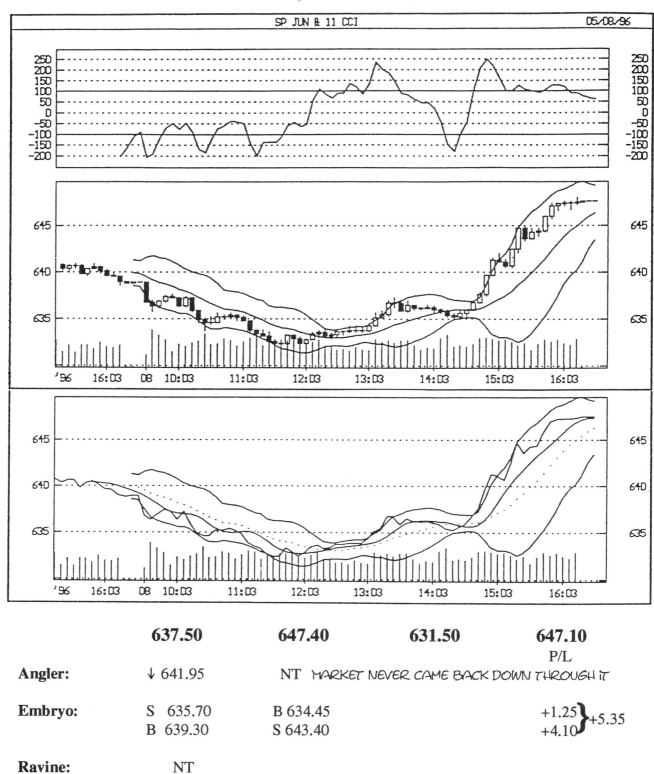

	637.50	647.40	631.50	647.10
				P/L
Angler:	↓ 641.95	NT MARKET NEVER CAME BACK DOWN THROUGH IT		
Embryo:	S 635.70	B 634.45		+1.25 } +5.35
	B 639.30	S 643.40		+4.10
Ravine:	NT			

Comment: There was a little too much action around 13:09 for a true **Ravine**. However, a case could be made for an upside breakout. Note upside **Staircase**.

Keeping a trading diary is such an important part of acquiring a consistent and effective trading plan that it becomes **Golden Rule #3 - *Keep a trading diary***. In practice, I keep two trading diaries, one a trade-by-trade record with charts of the trades actually made, the second a general overview diary which includes observations on the general market, individual stocks, sector funds, etc. Having a quote service/software combination makes it possible to print up charts in any of the available time frames with any of the available indicators. These can then be studied at leisure. One final mistake, in this section, to avoid, having kept a diary, is not to return to it frequently to see how one's perceptions and skills have changed---if they have---since the original entry.

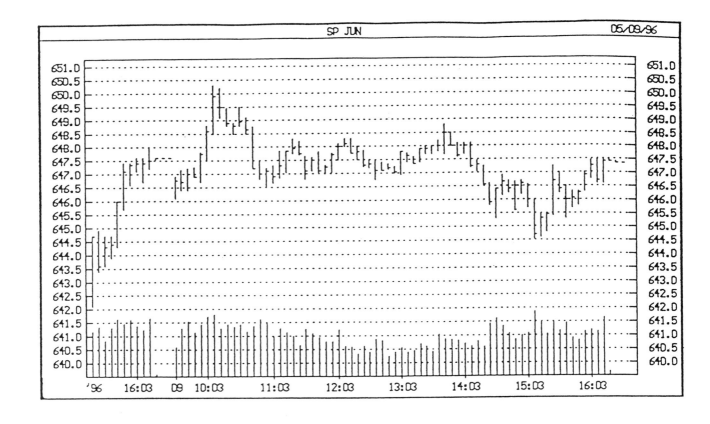

This is a bar chart.

POINT AND FIGURE SIGNALS

The Basic **BUY**

```
      Ⓧ
  X   X
  XOX
  XOX
  XO
  X
  X
```

The Basic **SELL**

```
  O
  O
  O
  OX
  OXO
  OXO
  O   O
      Ⓞ
```

Learning To Predict The Market
#1 From the Action of the Market Itself

Charts

The Basics

Charts make it possible to visualize relationships, which would not be obvious without them. There are four main forms of charting the movement of stocks, bonds, commodities or any of their indices.

1. **Bar Charts:** The type of chart familiar to anyone with even the most peripheral interest in following markets. These are by far the most common form of charts. They are featured in both *WSJ* and *IBD*.

2. **Point & Figure Charts:** This is a technique that has a long market history. If the market can advance X's are put above each other in a column. Each X represents an advance say of 10 units. The value of the size of the box filled by each X is decided by the trader. As the market advances, X's accumulate in the boxes. Note the numbers are opposite the center of the box. If the market can close 30 units below the base value of the last X box (a market that closes at 399.95 has a base value of 390 as it has not closed over 400) — so in this case if the market can close at or below 360 (390-30) we have a 3 box reversal (3 boxes each valued at 10 units). A new column is started **immediately to the right** of the X column 1 box below it. O's are entered in this column. The pattern formed by the alternating columns of X's and O's form buy and sell signals, the most basic of which are shown. Point and figure charts are popular with floor traders who follow the market tick-by-tick.

I use point and figure charts on one of my market indicators — the Trend Indicator — and get some great long term signals. I have not used them for futures trading as I really go for candlestick charts.

3. **Candlestick Charts:** These are often called Japanese candlestick charts, introduced almost single-handedly to the American trader by Steve Nison. [10] Steve's book is just marvelous-a *tour de force*. Basically, candlestick charts define precisely the range between the open and close---called the **real body** with the highs and lows added as **shadows**. Sometimes, of course, the high or low will be the open or close and the candle may be all real body with no shadows. Such candles have strong bullish or bearish significance.

I use candlesticks whenever I am not using **single point (SP) charts.** I would point out that candlestick charts enhance dramatically the information provided by regular bar charts. Not only do candlestick charts appeal to the eye, but they aid the eye in identifying relationships. And all the studies available on bar charts can be applied to candlestick charts. They are great. I urge you to use them. If you get involved with them, I know you will end up reading Steve Nison's book. But for our purposes, the basic candles are fine. A white candle is bullish-a black candle is bearish. It is that simple.

May 9, 1996

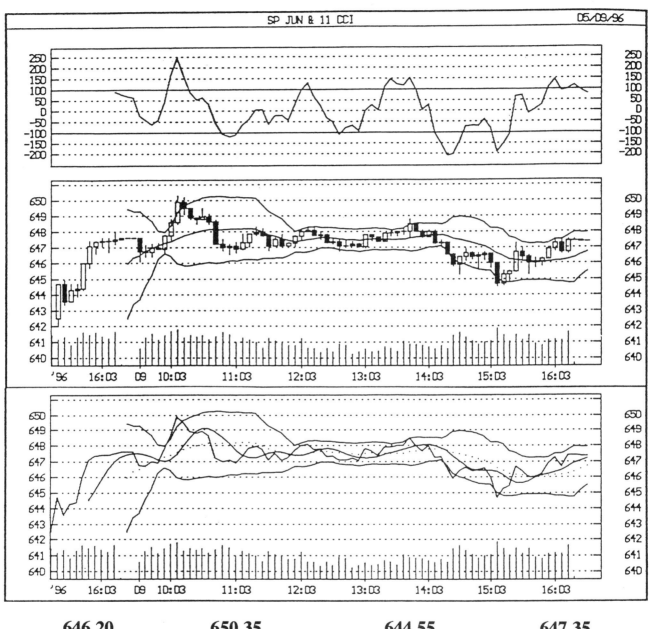

646.20	650.35	644.55	647.35

						P/L
Angler:	↑	646.35	B	646.35	S 649.05	+2.70
Embryo:	B	648.00	S	649.05		+1.05
Ravine:	S	646.60	B	645.85		+0.75

Comment: Great **Ravine** formation though not much profit. Sell signal #3 around 13:51.
(pg. 101)

4. **Single Point (SP) Or Close Only Charts:** I have used the single point method of charting for many, many years. The close of the selected time period is charted as a single point. It is the only value plotted from the time period in question. SP charts also clarify the picture and make drawing trendlines very easy. I use only SP charts and candlesticks.

So we have ways of plotting the action of any market we want to follow. Do we need anything else? Yes indeed. In 1992 John Bollinger came up with an idea that at first I did not like at all, as the bands looked untidy. John's idea was to take a moving average - he chose a 20 period simple MA and to run bands at ±2 standard deviations (S.D's) of the volatility, the range between high and low readings of the individual bars. These bands are known, not surprisingly, as *Bollinger Bands*. Ed Dobson wrote a good introduction to them *"Understanding Bollinger Bands."*[11]

Well, I don't know when I last ran a chart without Bollinger Bands, but it was not recently. As we shall see, I consider them essential. John selected a 20 period MA as the base for his bands. Being me I used a 21 period MA for a long time before settling on a 13 period MA as my regular length MA (with associated Bollinger Bands at ±2 SD's).

What To Expect

Charts can only tell you what has been. To the informed eye, they offer suggestions as to what may be, but it's important not to read your own feelings about the market into them when such an interpretation is not justified by the chart.

There are two significant events that have predictive value when they can be identified on a chart.

1. The Arrival of the Market at a Bollinger Band.

Let's consider a 6-minute candlestick chart of the S&P current contract. In order for the market to reach the upper Bollinger Band and close there, a white candlestick is a given. If the close is through the band and the upper band turns upwards, this observation has a strong predictive value, namely that the up movement will continue. I cannot give the exact percentage, but having identified the formation time and again I feel the chances of a further up move to be around 65-70%. It follows that a take-out of the high of this candle will provide a buy signal.

When the market arrives at a lower band, the exact reverse applies, and a sell signal will be generated by the market taking out the low of the candlestick bar.

ANATOMY OF A REVERSAL POINT (RP)

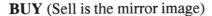

BUY (Sell is the mirror image)

Upper Bollinger Band

Market on single point (SP) chart arrives at and **closes** bar on Bollinger Band.

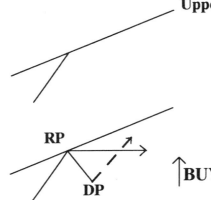

Close of new bar is below close of previous bar. A defining point (DP) has been formed.

THIS IDENTIFIES THE REVERSAL POINT (RP)

Important:

RP's of course form away from Bollinger Bands as well as at them. For a buy (not one of my official buy signals) the take-out point of the RP must occur **above** triangular MA7 though it may actually form below it.

Take-out is **above** TMA7

2. The Take-Out of a Reversal Point (RP)

Reversal points occur on single point charts. Let's consider an upward move in the market. At the end of the bar, the close will be at a particular value. Again we will use 6-minute charts. If, at the close of the next 6-minute bar, the value is lower than that of the original bar, then not only a **reversal point** (RP) but a **defining point** (DP) will have been formed. If the market now takes out the original RP, a **buy** signal is generated. Three entry techniques are available.

1. The take-out of the RP value plus 1 tick during the bar

2. The take-out of the high of the RP bar during the bar

3. The take-out of the RP value at the close of the bar

Obviously, you will have to toggle between candlestick and SP charts. I would like to mention the Ross Hook. [12] A Ross Hook occurs in an uptrending market on a bar chart when a lower high is formed. It is perfectly possible to get an RP without a lower high on the DP bar. All we need is a lower close. This is an important distinction between an RP and a Ross Hook.

Exactly the same formation occurs in reverse for a **sell** signal.

RP signals occur anywhere on the chart. The ones to look for are those that occur above the triangular 7 moving average for buys and below it for sells.

Obviously, the market is sending a pretty strong message when an RP formation occurs at a Bollinger Band. This combination signal often occurs around 2 PM on a day when the market has been down in the morning. I call this combo formation the *Sign of the Bull*. Preceding it, I demand a higher low as the market changes direction. This is a given most of the time. There is also an opposite sign, the *Sign of the Bear*. This is preceded by lower highs. (pg. 98)

There are two other formations that set up nicely on SP charts. If we consider the characteristic buy formation, it may at times turn into a sell formation. The buy is received (just) on the original set up. After the buy is received, the defining point (DP) for the buy setup becomes the RP for a sell setup. This is a **stop and reverse** (SAR) signal at the DP = RP. And of course just the reverse situation occurs on the downside when the original sell signal transforms into a buy.

Mistakes To Avoid

Single points only form at the close of a bar. A mistake to be avoided is to enter when you see a good looking formation and act on it **during** the bar. This is a 'now you see it, now you don't' situation. It takes a while to accept that a perfect situation that you saw on your computer screen during the course of the bar wasn't really there at all as a valid pattern and certainly will not show up on your charts when you print them at the end of the day. When M & W formations occur, it is often advantageous to stop and reverse on take-out of the middlepoint. This is one of the few times that SAR can be given as a single order.

M & W FORMATIONS

These occur on single point **(SP)** charts only. They also can be easily identified on any indicator that plots a single value for the close of the bar. (CCI and RSI are examples).

M FORMATION

An RP & DP occur in an up move

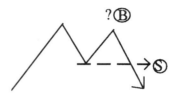

A possible buy signal is given with no follow through. **Sell** (again not an official signal) the take-out of the DP.

W FORMATION

An RP & DP occur in a down move.

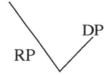

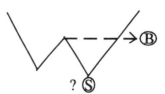

A posssible sell signal is given with no follow through. **Buy** the take-out of the DP.

#2 From Indicators

The Basics

Indicators are, by their very nature, late. By far the commonest indicator is a moving average. A 13 bar moving average totals up the average of the last 13 bars. A simple 13 bar moving average relates the average value to bar 7, with six bars in front of it and six behind it. It is in fact six bars "late."

Obviously, the shorter the time span of an indicator, the more up-to-date it will be. But also the whippier it will be. That said, let's examine the indicators I have found to be of value.

2-1) Moving Averages

There are a number of ways to calculate moving averages. We will consider three of them.

a) Simple MA's

A simple MA is just that, an average of the last X number of bars. When a new bar is formed, the old one, x number of bars back, is dropped. The result is a smoothing of the data. A number of systems use the market crossing a MA or a shorter MA crossing a longer one to generate signals. In order to weight the data to reflect more accurately the most recent data, exponentially weighted MA's may be used.

b) Exponential MA's (EMA's)

The simplest way to explain exponential MA's is to show how a 0.3 exponential MA is derived. A 0.3 EMA is roughly equivalent to a 6 day EMA. If you want to run a 0.3 EMA on a calculator, you will need to run a simple 6-day MA first. This will give you a starter figure of say 647.17. The 0.3 EMA is very easy to calculate. Now on day 7 the market on a daily basis closes at 655.00. Three-tenths (0.3) times the difference between this value and the starter value of 647.17 is applied to the starter value respecting plus and minus signs. This is the new 0.3 EMA with a value of 649.52.

$$(655.00 - 647.17) \times 0.3$$
$$7.83 \times 0.3 = 2.35$$
$$647.17 + 2.35 = 649.52$$

The same process repeated each day for 7 or 8 days will stabilize the 0.3 EMA. That's all there is to it. I recommend keeping daily charts by hand and updating the 0.3 EMA by calculator as doing so will provide a "feel" for the market not obtainable in any other way.

But if you are going to use a real-time data feed and trade bars of only a few minutes duration, there is no practical way to do this without having a software program that can calculate and draw the values.

MAY 10, 1996

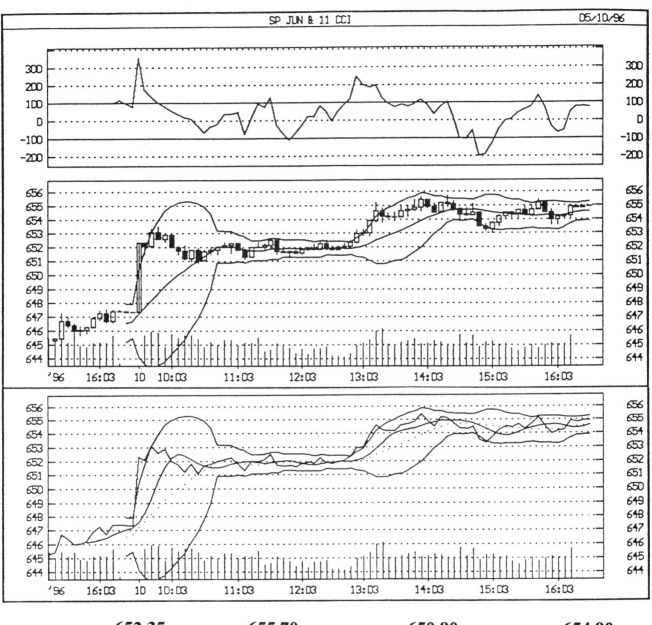

	652.35	655.70	650.90	654.90
				P/L
Angler:	↑ 646.75	NT		
Embryo:	B 654.15	S 655.15		+1.00
Ravine:	B 653.25	S 654.25		+1.00

Comment: I chose the take-out of the high of the second candle for entry. It is clear that an entry stop using the Bollinger Upper Band would have been lower (around 652.75).

c) Triangular MA's

One day I noticed a box labeled **triangular** in the moving average section of the MetaStock™ 4.52 RT program. Although I had been trading since 1958, I had never heard of triangular MA's. Here is what they are, as I learned from the excellent manual that comes with the MetaStock™ program.[13]

Triangular MA's are weighted MA's as are exponential MA's. The difference between them is that while exponential MA's give most weight to the most recent data, triangular MA's assign the majority of the weight to the middle portion of the data. This results in further smoothing of the simple MA data. I really like the smooth MA produced by this additional step and I use triangular MA's now most of the time I use MA's with real time data.

2-2) Commodity Channel Index (CCI)

After moving averages---the main indicator---I will consider the other indicators I use in alphabetical order. The CCI was described by Donald Lambert in 1980 (in *Commodities Magazine*, now renamed *Futures*). As detailed in the *MetaStock™ Users Manual*, CCI calculates the difference the mean price of a commodity and the average of the means over the time period (number of bars) chosen. This difference is then compared to the average difference of the time period. A factor is applied so that most of the readings fall within a range of ±100.

Signals are given as follows.

Buy

The index penetrates -100 from below.
        and/or
A positive divergence with the market occurs. (The indicator advances ahead of the market.)

Sell

The index penetrates +100 from above.
        and/or
A negative divergence with the market occurs. (The indicator declines ahead of the market.)

I really like CCI as it is somewhat quicker than other indicators. This means it works well on the longer time frames---say 45 min. bars that I use for options. I use an 11 bar CCI routinely as in the charts displayed. Notice the buy and sell signals in May '96.

MAY 13, 1996

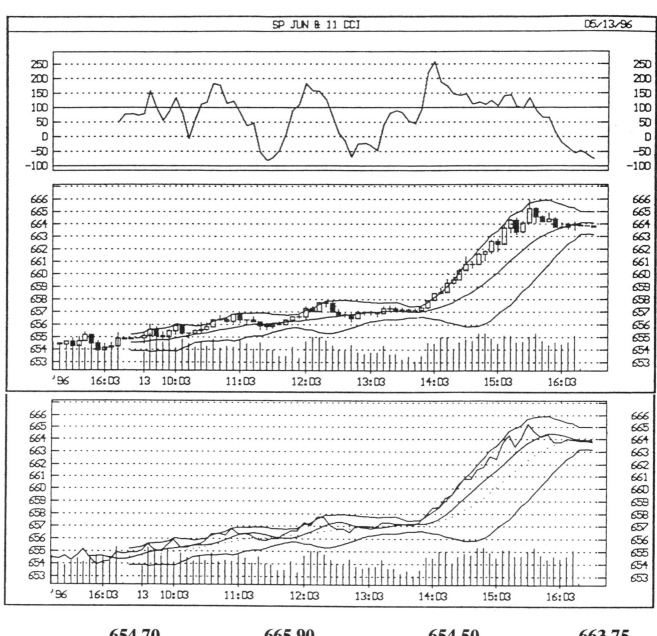

	654.70	665.90	654.50	663.75
				P/L
Angler:	↑ 651.85	NT		
Embryo:	B 655.50	S 657.25		+.75
Ravine:	B 658.95	S 664.55		+5.70

Comment: <u>Embryo</u>, If given more room, could have gained +8.15.
      <u>Staircase</u>, Also would have been highly successful.

2-3) MACD (MAC-D)

This indicator was invented by Gerald Appel. Jerry has written numerous books on the market and is editor-in-chief of *"Systems & Forecasts,"* [14] a stock market advisory which always ranks well in *Hulbert's Financial Digest.* [15] This service monitors the performance of all stock market newsletters.

MACD stands for moving average convergence/divergence indicator. It is calculated by taking the difference between the 0.15 and 0.075 exponential moving averages and running a 0.2 EMA as the signal line. Penetration of the signal line to the upside is a **buy**, to the downside a **sell**.

MACD, because of the way it is derived, is definitely one of the slower indicators, lagging the market more than the CCI for example. It also suffers from whipsawing on those occasions when the market is in a trading range.

One of MACD's strengths is that it defines the trend very nicely and allows for the inevitable counter-trend moves without triggering a change in trend prematurely.

MACD can also be plotted as a histogram with values above and below the zero line.

May 17-23, 1996

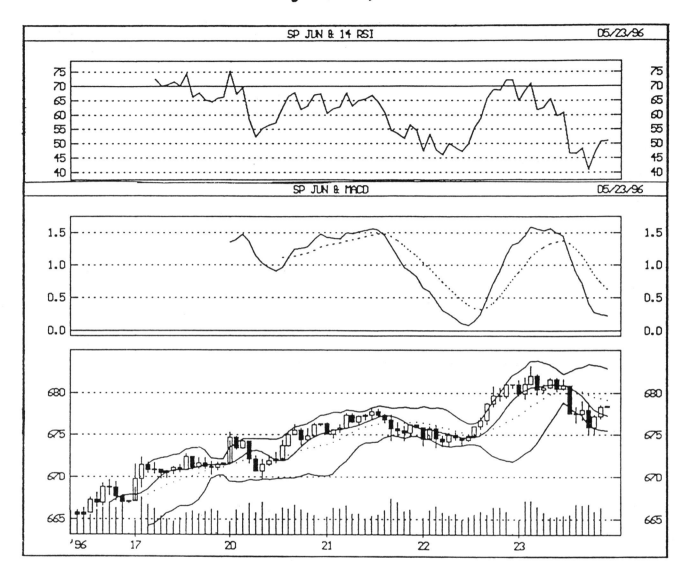

14 Bar RSI plus MACD

30 minute chart

Comment: Wilder uses a 14 bar RSI.

2-4) Relative Strength Index (RSI)

This indicator is the brainchild of J. Welles Wilder, Jr. It was revealed in his book *New Concepts In Technical Trading Systems* [16] which I took with me to the Bahamas on vacation in 1979. I recognized immediately the value of indicator for what it provided: a unique way to compare the action of the market to itself. It has been a major indicator of mine ever since. Indeed, it is the base indicator for the *Relative Strength Locator (RSL) System.*[1]

Briefly, if the market advances, so will the indicator and vice versa. The indicator shines at picking up divergences between the action of the market itself and the action of the indicator.

For trading S&P futures I use an 11 bar RSI. Besides bullish and bearish divergences, I look for formations similar to those I described under single point charts.

What To Expect

A number of false signals (as with any indicator).

Mistakes To Avoid

The most important mistake to avoid using RSI is one based on a lack of realization that the indicator runs "out of room" at the top and bottom of its range. When the market is running very strongly in either direction, the indicator will run out of room in the direction the market is headed, so a bullish or bearish "divergence" will be set up. It is not a true divergence, just the way the indicator responds to a very fast market. So a position taken on "divergence" is almost bound to fail and be costly.

2-5) Stochastics (Stokes)

Stochastics are the brainchild of George Lane. Their derivation is a bit complicated, but the values are based on a simple concept. As the market advances, the close of the bar will be nearer the high of the bar than the low of the bar. Indeed, if the advance is really strong, the close of the bar will also be the high of the bar. A higher close causes the indicator to advance, and just the reverse happens on the downside.

% **K Periods** - the number of bars used
% **K Slowing Periods** - the number of bars used to cause internal smoothing of % K
% **D Periods** - the number of bars used to form an exponential MA of % K.

These three values are all variable so the trader is left with a plethora of choices (which tends to lead to indecision). Notice the difference in timing between the default values 5-3-3 and 11-7-4. I usually use 11-7-4. (11=% K, 7=% K slowing, 4=% D)

May 23, 1996

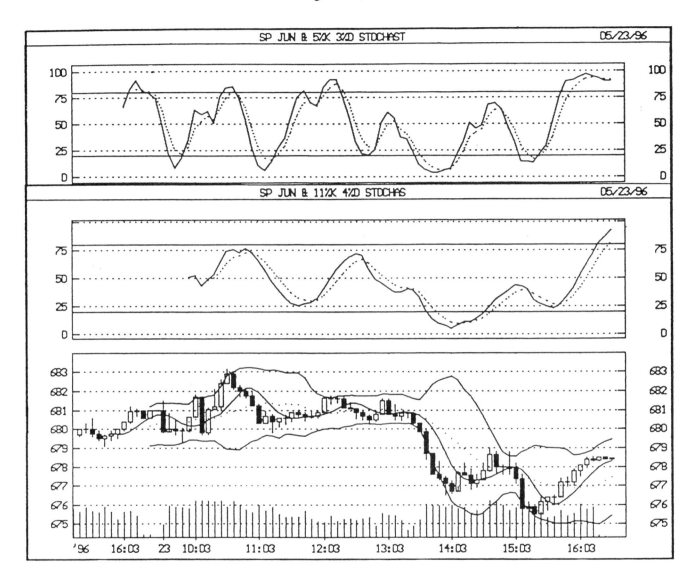

STOCHASTICS

5-3-3 compared to 11-7-4

Mistakes To Avoid

Never take a stoke buy when the market is falling sharply, and never take a stoke sell when the market is roaring ahead.

There are many, many other indicators out there. The ones I have described should suffice. Just remember, *1) indicators are late, 2) they should be used to confirm market action rather than as primary signals.*

There are times, I know, when entry is justified on the action of the indicator on its own, but such occasions are rare and, as a general rule, indicators are better looked on as providing trading ideas rather than absolute trading signals.

There is one rule that will save costly trading mistakes — it is so important that it is **Golden Rule #4:** *Never take an indicator signal counter to a strongly trending market.* You have to wait for the speed of the MA rise or fall to slacken and level off before going the other way. It is also important to be aware of the influence of opening gaps. If there is a large opening gap, the MA indicator will, of course, move sharply in the direction of the gap based entirely on the gap opening. This should not be interpreted as a strongly trending moving average, and under this one circumstance it is permissible to go counter to what looks like a strongly trending MA because the market is not really in a trend (though a trend may develop). A trend is formed by a number of bars with overall movement in one direction.

What To Expect

Since indicators are by their nature late, their predictive value is limited, but by no means is it absent. The art of prediction lies in anticipation of an event yet to happen. If the SP chart sets up part of a W formation (see pg. 52) and your favorite indicator is setting up nicely in oversold territory, you can take two different courses of action.

1. You can predict the market will advance and buy it on anticipation of the move. Or

2. You can wait for the move to happen and go with it hoping there is enough steam left in it to be useful.

I prefer the second approach, but if you are correct using approach #1, your profits will be significantly more substantial.

May 20, 1996

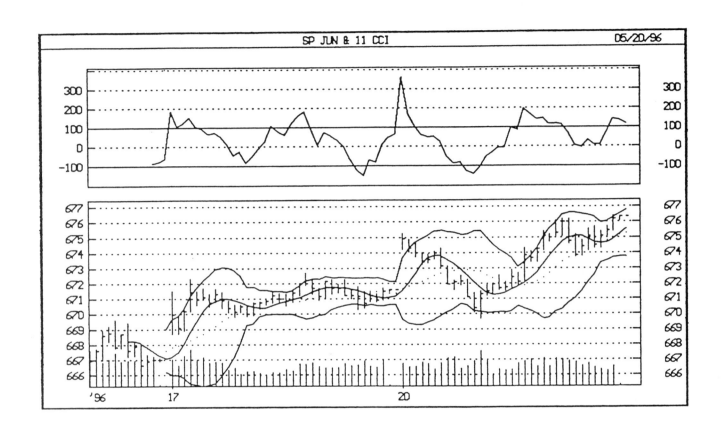

SP JUN & 11 CCI — 05/20/96

"Oops" Signal (Williams)

High of 5-17-96	672.70
Sell at	672.65

Mistakes To Avoid

We have discussed **Golden Rule #4**. Another mistake---one that is easy to make---is to read too much into an indicator. Indicators are complimentary to market action and only occasionally is a position to be taken primarily because of the action of an individual indicator. An example of this would be entry using stochastics on a day that looks like it is going to be what Gary Smith calls a "runner" or running day. We will consider such a day shortly.

#3 From Other Factors
3-1) Opening Gaps

Opening gaps occur frequently on the S&P, partly due to overnight trading on the Globex. The following observations may be of help.

Large Up Gap (More than 200-250 points) - Suspect that the gap will be filled. If the gap open occurs above the previous day's high, Larry Williams advises **selling** one tick below the previous high. He calls this pattern "Oops." My wife, Mary, learned about it from Larry in November of 1985 when she attended a Futures Symposium International given by Larry Williams, Bruce Babcock and Jake Bernstein in Chicago, *"Futures Trading By Computer."* This pattern has about a 65% success rate.

Smaller Up Gap (Less than 250-200 points) - When this happens, suspect the trend of the day will continue in the direction of the gap.

Limit Down Gap (The S&P has limit moves of 500 and 1200 points)[17] - Twice already in the first four months of 1996, the market has opened gap 1200 points down---in both cases being spooked by the bond market's reaction to the unemployment figures. Such gaps are, fortunately, unusual. They certainly grab the attention of those already long or the equally uncomfortable sellers of put options.

The first killer down gap in 1996 occurred on March 8 when trading resumed after a half hour's delay. The market came off its lows and entered a narrow trading range (**Ravine** pg. 87) before going into further free-fall.

The second killer down gap occurred exactly a month later on April 8. The market opened down 1200 points, fell another 800 points, then rallied back to close only 60 points below the open (though still of course 1260 points below the previous day's close). This gap took 15 trading days to fill completely while that of March 8 took 6 days. (pg. 22)

Feb 8, 1996

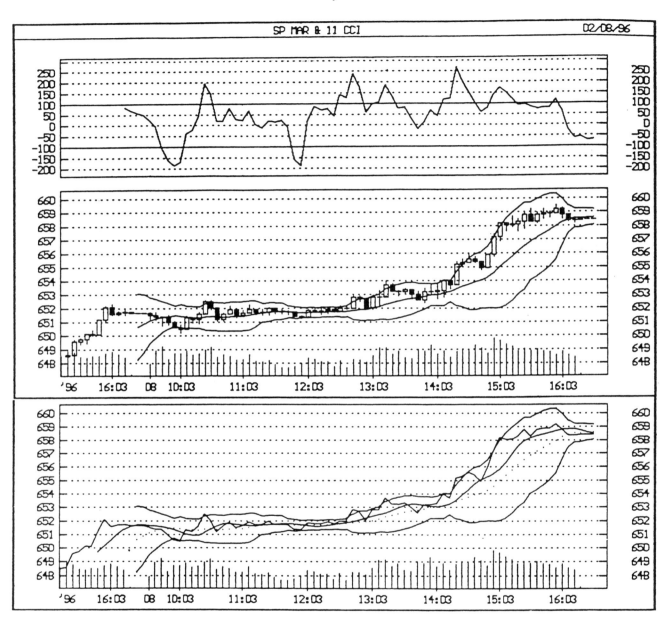

A Pure Up-Runner

Other Down Gaps

Large Gaps over 250 points have a tendency to reverse. If the gap is below the previous day's low, a Williams' Oops **buy** will be at one tick above the previous day's low. Smaller down gaps are variable, but be aware that a classic up running day may occur after a down opening gap (pg. 66). Also, one should be aware that gaps will not show up on SP charts nor on MetaStock™ candlestick charts. This is because the close of one bar is assumed to be the open of the next. If you want actually to see the gaps (rather than just be aware that they have occurred), then standard bar charts will be necessary. (pg. 62)

3-2) The Way the Day is Shaping Up

There are many patterns of behavior followed by the S&P. The most important are:

An up running day
A down running day
A pivot day
A chopper

An up running day — Every once in a while the market will start moving up and do so throughout the day. There may be a counter move around 2 p.m. that Ed Moore[18] calls "the contra" before the market continues up into the close. The clue to this day is the steady rise after 10:30 with only minor back off.

A down running day — A pure down runner is much rarer than a pure up runner. On a down running day the market may open on a down gap, work lower, hold during the middle of the day without much action either way, and then fall hard in the afternoon. A day that progresses ever downward is unusual.

A pivot day — This pattern is quite common. If the market is down in the morning, watch the action around 1:30 pm If the market makes higher lows start looking for the **Sign of the Bull** on a five or six minute time frame. This gives a very reliable signal and is formed on the SP chart when the SP value closes at the upper Bollinger Band. There is then a defining point below the SP close on the band. Buy the take-out of RP.

A pivot day may also occur with the market up in the morning. If the market enters into a flat low volatility time when absolutely nothing appears to be going on (**Ravine**), watch for a downside breakout. (Occasionally there may be a small and false upside breakout first.)

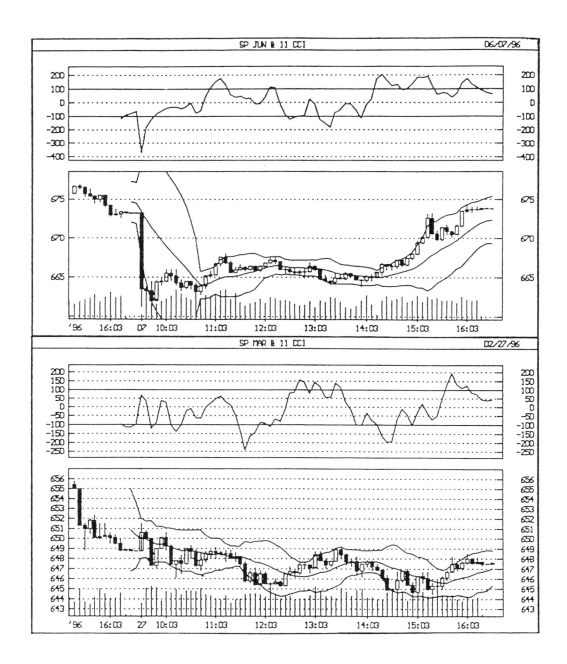

6-7-96   An **uprunner** after a large downside opening gap
2-27-96   A **chopper**

A chopper — As the name implies, the market chops back and forth changing direction two, three, or even four times during the day. Such days are difficult to predict early on, but a clue can be found in the pattern of the first hour to hour and a half's trading. Watch the candlestick charts. If white and black candles start alternating, suspect a chopper.

3-3) Government Reports

Your brokerage house will send you a list of the dates and times of all the reports that concern commodity traders. The market killer down gap on Monday, April 8 (pg. 86) was in response to the bond market's reaction to the unemployment report issued on Friday, April 5 - Good Friday - an exchange holiday. Other reports to watch are: *Leading Economic Indicators, Producer Price Index, Consumer Confidence Index, and Consumer Price Index.*

As far as I am concerned, the market will always find a reason to do something I, for one, am not expecting. And to judge by the action of the S&P into the close of Thursday, April 4, the other players were not expecting such behavior either. This is one of the great advantages of day trading — you cannot get caught on the wrong side of a large opening gap, but by the same token, you cannot profit from any action either.

Larry Williams uses an exit technique he calls **bail out**. He exits on the first profitable opening after taking the trade. He doesn't worry about opening gaps-indeed, he uses them to his advantage, and I wouldn't worry about them either if I had made and kept the kind of money Larry has taken from the markets.

Government reports will help you to assess what may happen to the market. However, if the market gaps down 1200 points-that has happened - and there is nothing to be done except to note that some further downside action is almost a given; I think the real value of the reports is knowing when they are due out so that new positions can be avoided immediately in front of a report that traders believe to be of importance.

3-4) Interest Rates and the Bond Market

I do not understand bonds --- or maybe I should say I do not understand bond traders. Well, I understand them enough to know that if things look good, bond traders worry they will get too good and trigger inflation. So they knock bonds down.

May 14, 1996

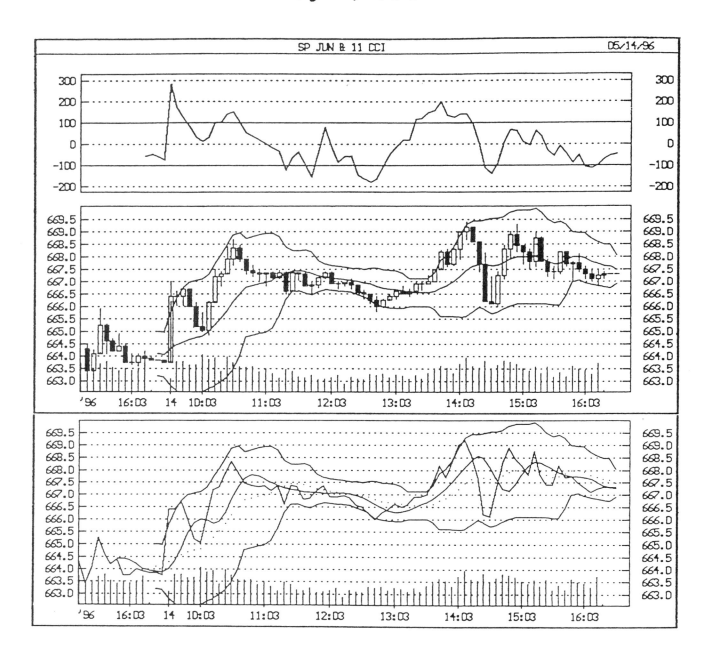

	667.00	669.40	664.85	667.30
			P/L	

Angler: ↑ 658.50   NT

Embryo: S 665.20   B 666.45   −1.25 }   −2.50
         B 668.80   S 667.55   −1.25

Ravine: NT close, but no cigar

Comment: Embryo bombed. Sold close to low. Bought close to high. It happens.

Sometimes the stock market and S&P futures move lock step with the bond market. At other times they uncouple. One of these days, I will have the bonds ticking away, doing their thing on the screen at the same time that the S&P's are doing their thing. Ed Moore follows both throughout the day and tells me he can anticipate moves in the S&P's by watching what bonds are doing. Presently I am reluctant to pay the additional monthly exchange fees (to the Chicago Board of Trade). Also, I like to see the S&P's full screen or with just one indicator.

But this I do know — if interest rates begin to rise and continue to do so, that is bad news for both the stock and bond markets.

3-5) Premium or Discount of Futures to Cash

The S&P index---the cash market---has been in existence for a very long time. S&P futures trading off the S&P cash index only became a reality in April 1982. There are 4 different contracts -March-June-September-and December. When the December contracts **expire on the third Friday in December**, the value of the December contract will exactly equal that of the cash market. But during the life of the December contract the futures contract will trade, usually at premium to, occasionally at discount from the cash index. It is the distortion of the normal fair value of premium of the futures to cash that triggers **program trading**.

Let's imagine the S&P cash is trading at 650.00 and the present futures contract---the next one to expire---is trading at 655.00. This premium, 500 points to cash, is above fair value (the assessment of 'fair' value is subjective, but it is safe to say that a current contract with, say, two months left until expiration, with a premium of 500 points over the cash value, would be considered overvalued). Enter the program traders. They know if they buy a basket of stocks to parallel the S&P cash index and sell stock futures, they will lock in a profit as at expiration the futures premium---presently at 500 points premium to cash---will have disappeared so the 500 points is theirs to keep no matter what happens to the cash market

S&P index now	650.00
S&P futures now	655.00
<u>At Expiration</u>	
S&P index	645
S&P futures	645
S&P index loss	500 points
S&P futures gain	1000 points
(from sale)	
Net gain	500 points

May 15, 1996

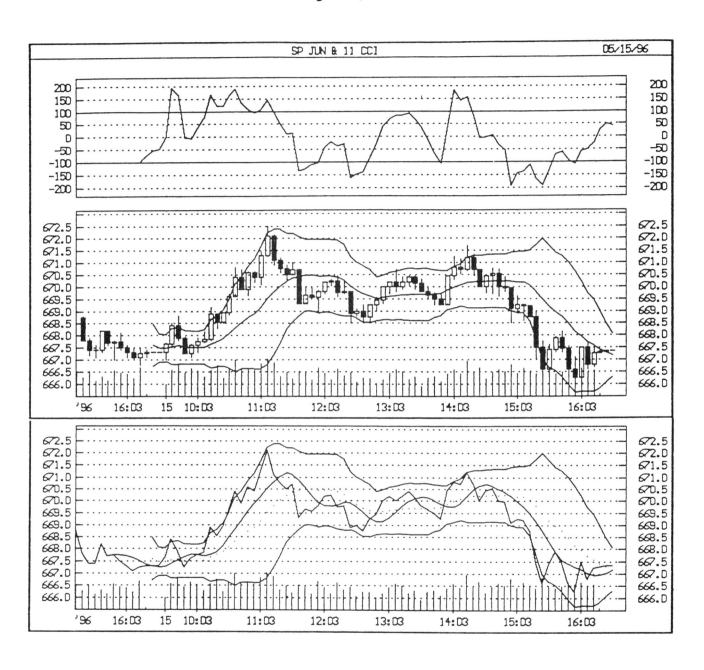

667.50	672.50	666.15	667.35
		P/L	

			P/L
Angler:	↑ 662.40	NT	
Embryo:	B669.30	S670.30	+1.00
Ravine:	NT		

Comment: When a black candle (11:03 - 11:09) engulfs the real body of a preceding white candle expect a reversal.

So if premium gets excessive, buying will occur in the cash market and selling in the futures market. Usually the effect of the former will outweigh the latter and the market will advance. But what happens to the futures is that some of the premium will be lost, so short term the futures may decline. What is certain is that the premium will return to or towards fair value and this fact has predictive value.

On the other side of the equation, when the premium declines to under-valued or a discount of futures to cash occurs, program traders will buy futures and sell stocks. And if there are no buyers out there looking for stock bargains, the general market will go into free-fall as it did on October 19, 1987.

3-6) Tick & Trin

The Tick Index is a stock market indicator used to show strength or weakness in the market. If more stock trades occur on upticks---that is, at a price higher than the previous trade-than on downticks, the market is showing strength which can be measured by the combined numbers. Values over +200 or so are bullish -200 bearish. **The Tick Index** is featured on CNBC's tape. Gary Smith finds it and the Trin useful in his trading.

The Trin or Traders Index is a reciprocal indicator. Values below 0.90 are bullish---more than 1.10 are bearish. I look at the ticker before making a trade. I like to see both in bullish territory if I am thinking of buying and both bearish if selling. But that's about it. For the more advanced interpretation of Tick and Trin and the interpretation of the action of other averages such as Dow transports, utilities and NASDAQ, I have to refer you to Gary's book. He examines the interaction and predictive value of these markets and indicators in great detail. Beware though of having too many factors involved in the decision-making process. There will always be one factor suggesting no go. Don't talk yourself out of a good trade. You can never, for practical purposes, get all the pieces in exactly their ideal positions on the board, and you are not going to make any money unless you make a move---known as pulling the trigger.

May 16, 1996

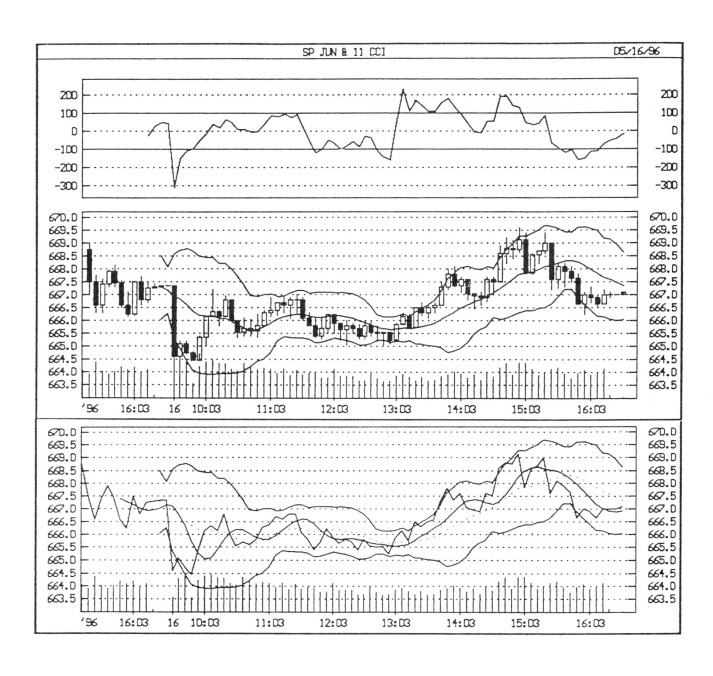

663.80	669.60	663.60	667.05
		P/L	

				P/L	
Angler:	↑ 663.90	B 663.90	S 665.95	+2.05	
Embryo:	B 665.60	S 666.60		+1.00	
Ravine:	NT				

Comment: There is a negative divergence on the CCI at 15:03

72

3-7) Globex

This is the overnight worldwide electronic market run by the Chicago Mercantile Exchange. Only limit orders (price or better) are accepted. Trading in index futures, currencies, bills and bonds occurs with only a short break between the day session and the night session.

For the S&P futures, the night session runs from 3:45-8:15 Chicago time which is 4:45-9:15 EST. There is therefore only a 15-minute break between the night session and the day session.

For day-traders, what happens on the Globex overnight is of minor importance as day traders do not carry a position overnight. But position traders not only cannot ignore the Globex, but should probably be trading it, certainly around the time of significant reports. (It is trading on the Globex overnight that causes those large opening gaps in the currencies and also, from time to time, the S&P's.) Knowing what happened overnight on the Globex can help prepare one's mind for likely scenarios in the day session.

A final point---when figures for the previous day's trading are published in newspapers, the Globex close may be used as that day's open. **What you need for *Trophy* and other systems is the first opening print for the day session that you see on your computer screen.**

3-8) The Pivot Numbers

The so-called pivot numbers are derived as follows. Take the mean of the previous day's high low and close, and use these numbers to predict the next day's high and low.

$$\text{High} \quad \text{Low} \quad \text{Close}$$

Example: 665.80 662.45 663.15

$$\text{Mean is } \frac{665.80 + 662.45 + 663.15}{3}$$

$$= 663.80$$

Tomorrow's predicted **high** = 2 x mean - previous low

$$= 1327.60 - 662.45$$

$$= \textbf{665.15}$$

predicted **low** = 2 x mean - previous high

$$= 1327.60 - 665.80$$

$$= \textbf{661.80}$$

Also, there are two other values called outer high and outer low. These are found as shown.

May 17, 1996

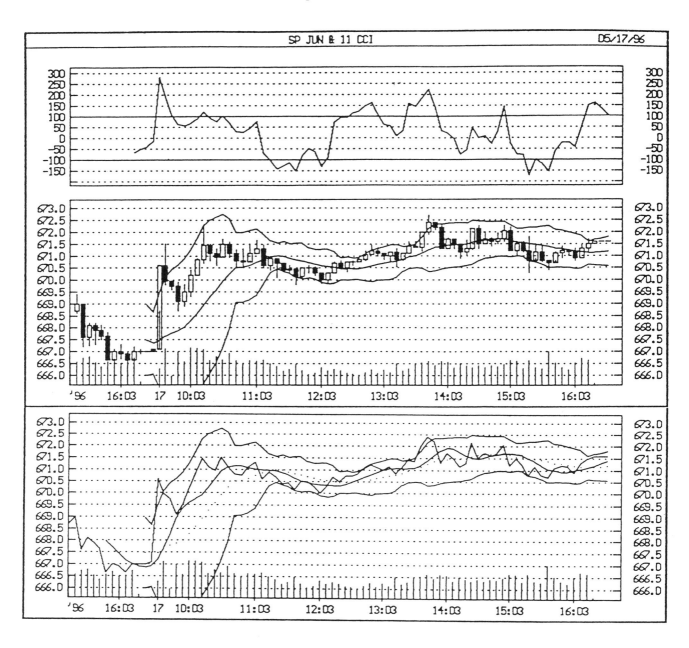

668.70	672.70	668.70	671.60
		P/L	

			P/L
Angler:	↑664.75	NT	
Embryo:	B 670.50	S 671.50	+1.00
Ravine:	NT		
Comment:	Early action fizzled. This is not rare.		

Outer high = mean - predicted low + predicted high

$\qquad$ = 663.80 - 661.80 + 665.15

$\qquad$ **= 667.15**

Outer low = predicted low - (predicted high - mean)

$\qquad$ = 661.80 - (665.15 - 663.80)

$\qquad$ **= 660.45**

The importance of these numbers is that the predicted high is thought to act as resistance. If taken out, the outer high is then the next resistance level, and if the market just keeps on going, well so much for the pivot numbers.

The projected low and outer low are looked on as support areas---maybe.

So know where the numbers are since other traders use them, but do not trade off them on their own.

So these are the ways that I know of to try and predict what the market will do. As a pathologist, I had to be substantially correct close to 100% of the time as people's health and lives depended on my diagnoses. Diagnosis means to know thoroughly. It is important to realize that the market ---any market, be it the S&P market, gold, coffee or anything else---can never be known with any thing close to finite accuracy; 65-70% accuracy is outstanding. Some systems have an accuracy rate of under 50%, but do well as the winners are far larger than the losers.

We have now to discuss how to set about trading futures and we should start with money management. Money management is as important as a good trading strategy or trading system. Indeed, I've heard it said that good money management coupled with a mediocre system will beat poor money management and a really good system.

MONEY MANAGEMENT

Money management relates to keeping the ball in play. It means not going for broke on a shot (trade) that has a low percentage possibility of success. It means limiting the amount of capital risked on a trade to a reasonable percentage of the equity in the account.

Presently the **margin**, or good faith money, that has to be in the account in order to trade the S&P has to be $15,120. But this applies to overnight trades. For day-trades only, the margins are less---exactly how much less will depend on the brokerage house you use and their assessment of you, but around $6,000-$7,000 should be sufficient.

May 20, 1996

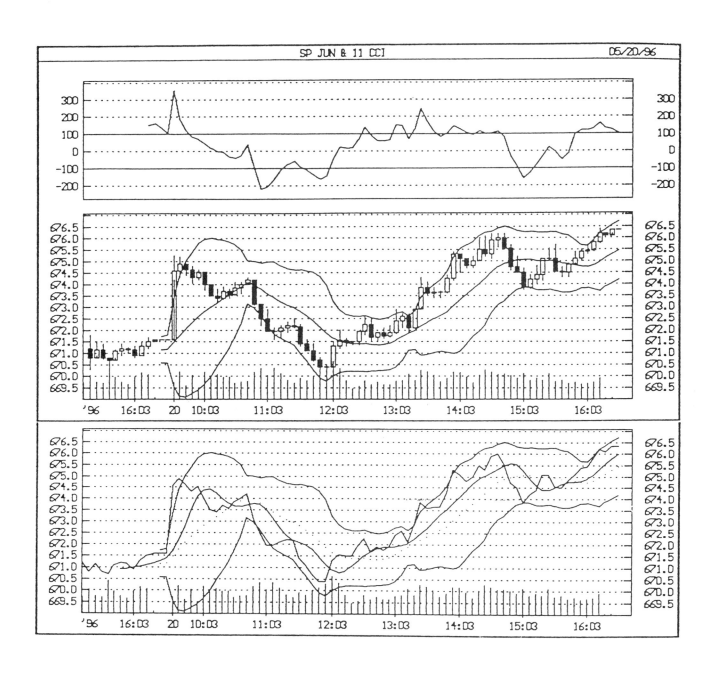

675.00	676.40	669.70	676.25
		P/L	

			P/L
Angler:	↑ 668.40	NT	
Embryo:	S 673.20	B 672.20	+1.00
Ravine:	NT		
Comment:	An *Oops* Signal occurred at 672.65 (May 17 high less one tick)		

If the current S&P futures contract is trading at 650.00, this represents stock valued at $325,000 (650 x $500) for **one** contract. It is important to bear this in mind and not to feel 'small' when ordering up one contract. You have just given an order controlling 32.5% of a million dollars. A move of 1% up or down would be valued at $3,250 or 650 points ($6.50). Now a move of 1% is a pretty small move, whereas a loss of $3,250 is a big loss. This is what, among other factors, makes trading the S&P so difficult. I believe that the account equity to trade one S&P contract should be 10% of the value of the contract, that is $32,500. I accept, however, that the average trader does not start a trading account with this much capital. But I further believe that one should never risk more than $900 (180 points) max on any one trade. **Slippage** and **commissions** may mean the loss at times approaches or even exceeds $1,000. If you start with a $20,000 account, this represents 5% of your capital. These figures should be your guidelines. If you drop your stop size to $500, you of course reduce the amount of capital at risk. But be warned, this may increase, not decrease, the overall losses.

So here are my rules for money management.

1. A trade should start going your way almost immediately. If you do not show a profit after 4 or 5 bars---the actual amount of time of course depends on the time frame used---consider exiting the trade. You do not have to wait for your stop to be hit if the trade is not acting well. Indeed, if you exit at the market, you may decide to leave your erstwhile protective stop in---now as an entry stop in the other direction.

2. Never chase a losing trade, either by adding more money or moving your stop.

3. Identify a point to place your stop which, if reached by the market, will prove your assessment was wrong. If this is beyond the comfort zone, either skip the trade or use a money management stop.

4. Money management stops, of a fixed dollar amount, are less desirable than market stops (above) but easily beat having no stops at all.

5. Take only those trades with at least two positive and unrelated factors going for them---the high-probability trades.

6. Do not risk more than 5% of your capital on any trade.

7. Accept that losses are inevitable. Take them quickly.

8. Follow your trading plan. Do not switch around. Plan your trade---trade your plan.

9. After three losses in a row, take a trading break.

10. Remember to put the whole game in perspective. No one forces you to trade and if trading makes you too anxious, simply quit. There is no shame involved. Not everyone can walk on hot coals in their bare feet.

May 21, 1996

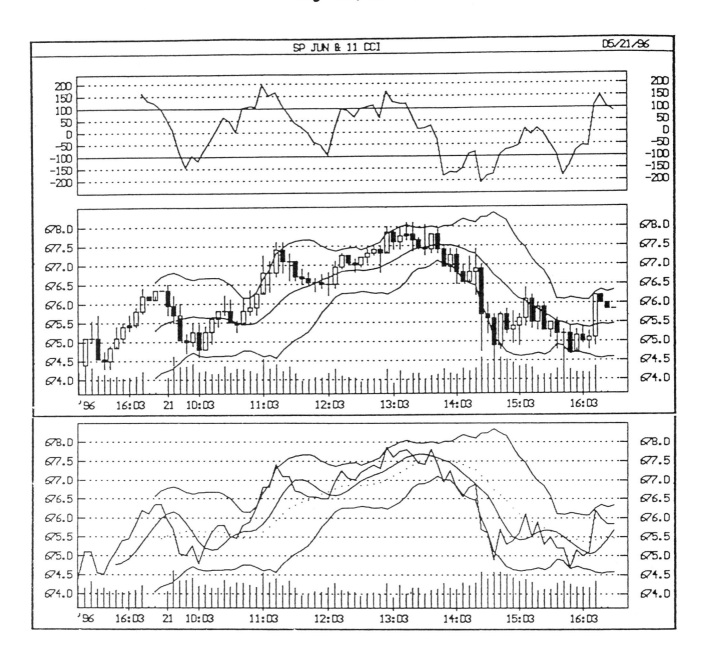

	676.40	678.10	674.30	675.85
			P/L	

Angler:	↑ 662.40	NT	
Embryo:	S 674.60	B 675.85	-1.25
Ravine:	NT		
Comment:	**Embryo** got stopped into the very lowest tick of the morning session. It happens.		

An integral part of money management is the placement of stops. I confess that I tend to put them too close to the action. I know I should give the market more room, but money management principle #1 is an important one. The ideal situation is *1) to call your order in, 2) to get filled and have the market go your way immediately, such that, 3) your stop can be a break-even or a profit protector.*

Be warned, though, if you put a stop within 30-35 points of the present market, the chances of it getting hit are really high. You would probably do better to exit "at the market." In fact, my experience is that 50 points is the minimum distance if you plan to try and stay in the trade. This will be usually as a stop to protect profit; a **protective stop**. A stop to prevent significant loss (a stop-loss) entered soon after the trade is under way should, in my opinion, not be closer than 75 points. Actually, the ideal money management stop is somewhere between 75 and 125 points plus an allowance for market "noise" of another 10-25 points. This is on a 3 to 6-minute time frame. Stops have to get somewhat larger as the time frame increases.

Stops are tricky to place and my advice is probably not the best there is. But I do know they have to be used. A very significant mistake to avoid is that of waiting to set your stop for several minutes after your order gets filled. The temptation is to wait quite a while to see what the market will do. The first time it may come down to your, as yet mental, stop and then ride right back up to a nice profit. The second or third time you avoid placing a stop however, expect the market to crash through the area where your stop should have been and just keep on going in the wrong direction, ultimately handing you a large loss. Jake Bernstein [19] calls this *"negative reinforcement."* In the first instance you were rewarded for doing the wrong thing; in the second you were punished.

May 22, 1996

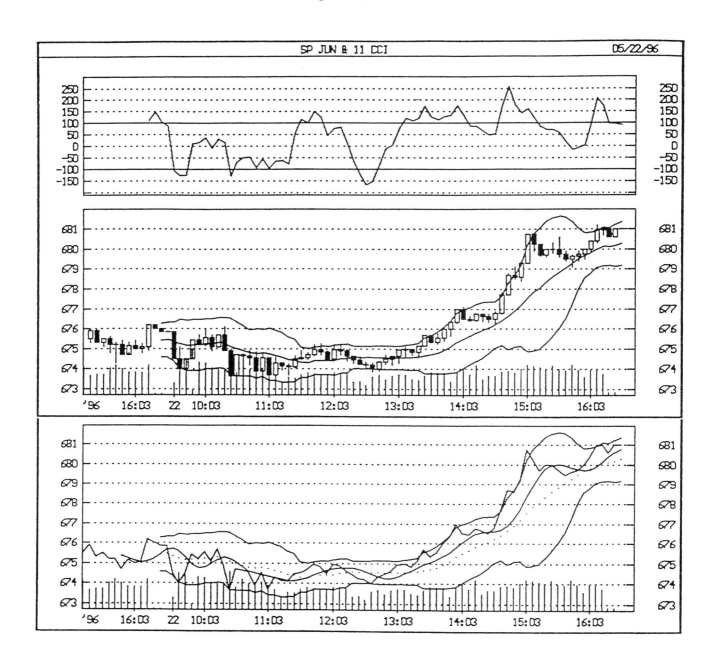

	674.80	681.20	673.50	681.00
			P/L	
Angler:	↑673.30	NT		
Embryo:	B 676.60	S 679.50	+2.90	
Ravine:	B 676.05	S 679.50	+2.45	

Comment: When the market is running strongly, **Angler** is usually inactive as the counter move necessary to set up the signal is large.

As we have already seen, stops can be used both to enter the market as well as exit it. *"Set-it and forget-it systems,"* by their very nature, are very likely to use stops for entry as the orders become too complicated otherwise. **Trailing stops** are often used for exit once a certain potential profit has been achieved. Gary Smith warns against trying to scalp a quick $200 to $300 profit. He believes in letting the market run until the close providing his 170 point trailing stop is not hit. He believes that those who try to scalp the S&P with tight stops either do not understand it or have a gambler's mentality.

Well, I have a great deal of respect for Gary, but I also believe if you position your trades correctly in relationship to the Bollinger Bands, you can do well trading with an in and out style. The choice is personal. Certainly, if you have a live data feed, I see no reason not to take small shots (chip shots if you like for the golfers who I hope are still with me).

Four Trading Patterns To Examine For The S&P

Trading 'systems' are usually highly priced and often come with non-disclosure agreements. The four trading patterns I am presenting here are not full-fledged systems, though I believe **Angler** and **Embryo** could each be worked up into a salable system. Presently none of the patterns have a real time track record and as the Commodity Futures Trading Commission and National Futures Organization require, I must warn you that the simulated performance results I am going to present are just that---simulated. The full warning and disclaimer are printed at the beginning of this manual and should be reread. The results for each pattern that might possibly have been achieved for each trading day during the month of May 1996 will be presented to give an idea of the effectiveness of the patterns.

1) Angler

Back under exponential moving averages, we considered the way a 0.3 EMA was derived. I noticed many years ago how well the 0.3 EMA tracks the market once the market starts trending. I know all MA's do nicely in trending markets, but the 0.3 EMA does well in picking up early a change either of trend reversal or trend to trading range.

As the market advances, the 0.3 EMA at first lags behind it. Indeed, the distance that the 0.3 EMA is from the market close helps decide that a trend is indeed under way.

0.3 EMA CHART FOR ANGLER

Angler Bait Point	Date April 30	Close 654.85	0.3 EMA 654.09	654.85 + 654.10 / 2 = May 1 Bait Point 654.50
654.50	May 1	656.45	654.80	
655.65	2	645.85	652.12	
649.00	3	643.50	649.53	
646.50	6	642.90	647.54	
645.25	7	638.95	644.96	
641.95	8	647.10	645.60	
646.35	9	647.35	646.13	
646.75	10	654.90	648.76	
651.85	13	663.75	653.26	
658.50	14	667.30	657.47	
662.40	15	667.35	660.43	
663.90	16	667.05	662.42	
664.75	17	671.60	665.17	
668.40	20	676.25	668.49	
672.40	21	675.85	670.70	
673.30	22	681.00	673.79	
677.40	23	678.45	675.19	
676.85	24	680.65	676.83	
678.75	28	673.80	675.92	
674.85	29	669.10	673.87	
671.50	30	673.40	673.73	
673.60	31	667.05	671.73	

Angler is a day-trading pattern based on the market close and the 0.3 EMA updated for the latest market close. Let's consider the close of May 2, 1996. The closing value was 645.85 with the 0.3 EMA at 652.12. The market was in a short-term downtrend as the market's close was **below** the 0.3 EMA.

The 0.3 EMA figure should now be rounded off to the nearest tick and the mean between it and the closing value found by adding them together and dividing by 2. This is the "bait." The value is 649.00 (rounded off).

In a downtrend (market below the 0.3 EMA), if the market **the following day** can **rise** 15 points (3 ticks) above the bait, this figure then becomes the entry stop to **sell** the market if it comes back **down** through that value.

The initial protective stop is 125 points. If the market declines 125 points (to give you a potential profit in a down market), move your stop to 75 points profit. If you have 150 points of profit, take 100 points. If you have 200 points of potential profit, make sure you get 125 points and if the market moves 250 points in your favor, trail the low with a stop 125 points above it. These profit parameters obey **Golden Rule #2**, but tend to leave a lot of money on the table. So experiment.

In an **up** market, the procedure is just the opposite---the mean of the close and the 0.3 EMA becomes the **buy** point if the market gets 15 points **below** the "bait," then comes up through it.

So what happened on May 3rd? I'm glad you asked---the market took off through the sell point of 649.00 to reach 650.70. It then came back down to trigger the 649.00 sell. Exit was at 639.50 + 1.25 = 640.75 for a theoretical profit of 825 points ($4125---see chart of May 3 pg. 32)

There are some points to be made about **Angler**.

1. It is based on the solid idea that a trend once established (and identified) will continue. **Angler** only takes trades in the direction of the trend. It uses small countertrend moves to set up the pattern.

2. It is important to give it some room to achieve worthwhile gain as in this example. That is why it is important to let the trade achieve 125 points of potential profit before moving the stop to 75 points profit (it is worth experimenting with these parameters).

3. If 100 points of potential profit have been received, the trader may decide to exit at break-even. Remember, this is a trading idea and pattern, not a rigid system.

May 23, 1996

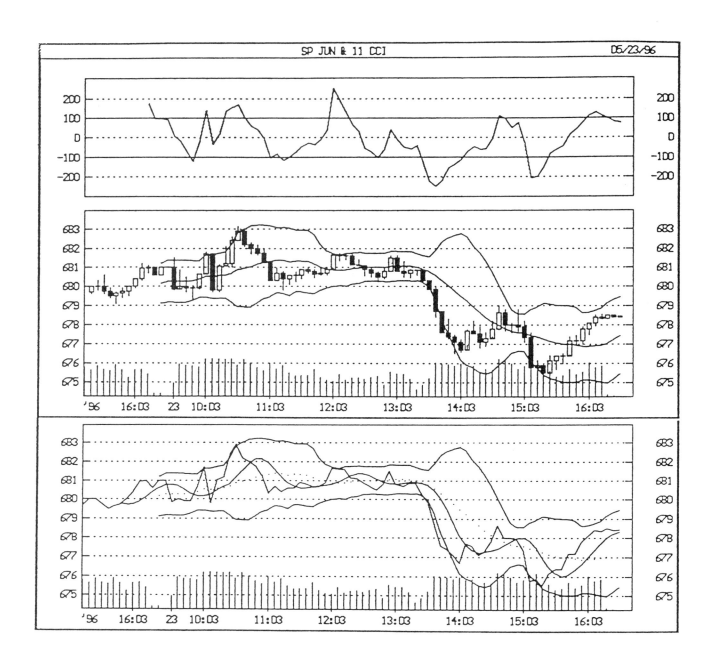

	681.50	683.15	675.10	678.45
			P/L	
Angler:	↑677.40	B 677.40	S 678.40	+1.00
Embryo:	S 679.70	B 677.75		+1.95
Ravine:	S 679.95	B 677.75		+2.20

Comment: Positive divergence on CCI late in the day. Probably too late to trade though there are some strong moves into the close.

In May 96 **Angler** achieved 1790 points of simulated profit. There were 7 wins and 1 loss. Allowing $100 (20 points) for slippage and commissions, this is a theoretical profit of $8,150. I do not have any substantial back data, and I stress I put this forward as a trading idea you may want to try out and experiment with. Other EMA's or some factor other than the mean between the close and the 0.3 EMA may give better results.

2) Embryo

The idea behind this pattern is both simple and logical. It is based on two observations; a) the open is frequently near the high or low of the day, b) wide range days with real bodies of 400 or more points have to start their run in a small way. You cannot get an up day of 600 points without an up value of say 200 points first.

All you have to do with **Embryo** is note the opening price — we need to use the first print of the day session (ignore overnight Globex values). Now enter a **buy stop** 180 points above and a **sell stop** 180 points below the open.

The exit stops are exactly as described for **Angler**. Note that when one stop is hit, you have to move the other to a value 125 points away. Let's say the market opens at 641.50.

Enter **buy stop** at 643.30

Enter **sell stop** at 639.70

If the buy stop gets hit, move the sell stop to 642.05 (643.30-1.25). This is your protective stop. If this gets hit, meaning you are out of the trade, reinstate the original sell stop---do not reinstate the original buy stop. That is all there is to this pattern. In a volatile market, it is a good way of snagging some profit. But be warned, trading range days will be tough. One way to filter trades is to use the pattern only on days with an opening gap of at least ±1.00.

Embryo gained 2435 points **after** slippage and commissions in May 96, much helped by the volatility of the market. There were 21 wins, 6 losses. This is a pattern with "runs" of winning and losing trades as shown by some back testing. One possibility is to take signals only after 12 Noon EST. But if you can get aboard one of those big days and stay with the trade, you will snag some real money.

April 8-11, 1996

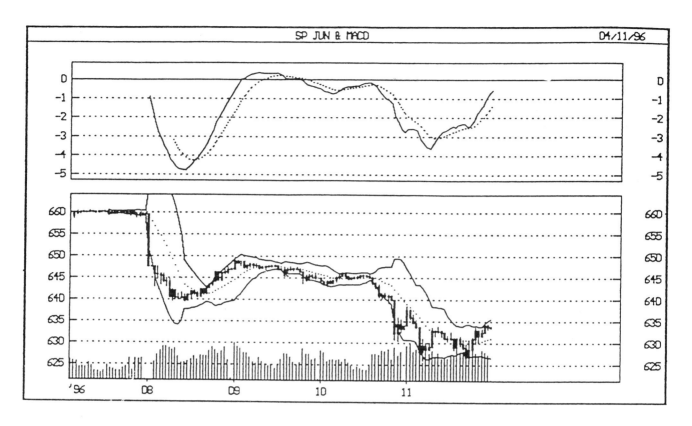

Ravine:

Like all good patterns, **Ravine** works on multiple time frames. This is a 15 minute per candle chart. Above is Jerry Appel's **MACD** giving, as you see, a nice buy during the day of April 8.

3) Ravine

This is not a common pattern, but it is a reliable one when it forms. Sometimes, usually around the middle of the day, the market just goes dead. There is little up or down movement in the market and the individual bars become shorter. In addition, the Bollinger Bands become flat and narrow. The chart now looks like a **Ravine** — a long, narrow area. Nothing is more sure than that the market will not stay there forever, or even for a protracted length of time. The **Ravine** formation should be of about two hours duration.

When you identify **Ravine**, you should aim to buy/sell the breakout. You can use the values of Bollinger Bands themselves (as they will be flat) or the highest/lowest value while in **Ravine** or the take-out of the candle following the candle that got you out of the ravine (to avoid false breakouts). Give each value 2 ticks.

As noted, this pattern is not common but has a high success rate. It should also be noted that the pattern may extend across more than one day (April 9 and 10 `96). In this case a well-defined ravine with diminished volatility (diminished, that is, compared to Apr. 8) was formed with subsequent downside breakout.

The results for May 1996 showed 9 wins 0 losses for a gain of 2310 points **after** slippage and commissions.

Finally, an idea that should make money any time the market runs up or down. The results---here we go again---simulated, theoretical, not actually taken, were so good for May 1996 that I have decided just to present the idea and hope you may profit from it, and not give details of the kind of money that could have been made during the merry, merry month of May. It is obvious, however, that some very significant profits were available.

4) Staircase

The pattern is based on a simple idea. If the market starts to run either up or down, it is much more likely to keep going in that direction than it is to reverse. Here is the setup.

1. Use a 3-minute chart (the only time I recommend 3-minute charts).

2. Wait for the market on an SP chart to close at (or through) a Bollinger Band.

3. Now watch the band that was hit.

May 8, 1996
STAIRCASE

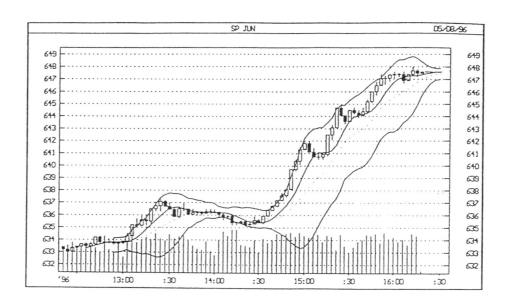

Going Up

3 Minute Charts

May 3, 1996

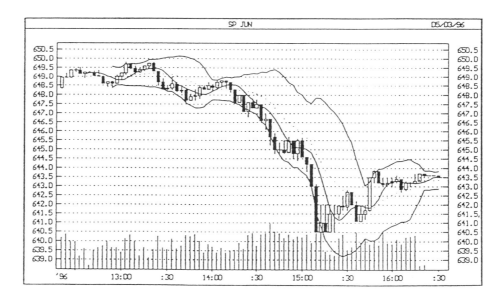

Going Down
Perhaps I should have called this pattern "*elevator*"

4. If the upper band turns up or has already turned up, you have a **buy setup**.

5. If the lower band turns down or has already turned down, you have a **sell setup**.

6. Enter on a stop at either the next whole number or the next 50 point mark, whichever is nearer.

7. Aim for a profit of 100-200 points with a protective stop of 100 points.

Note: You have a profit target of 100 to 200 points---the choice is personal. **If the market is really running, you may achieve the profit objective almost immediately. In this case, it is a good idea to let the trade run monitoring it with a triangular 7 bar MA of the closes.**

Staircase could have gained some spectacular profits on May 8 on both sides of the market (pg. 44). The market was down strongly in the morning, the Dow down 80 points or so---with a reversal around noon. The Dow closed up 53 points. This was the first time the 50 Dow point trading curbs, designed to limit program trading, were triggered on both the downside and the upside on the same day.

Staircase needs a running market. Do not try using it in any other kind of market. But in a running market, it does provide a way of getting aboard the move. In a strong move, reaction points may be few and far between. They represent an attempt by the market to retrace a previous move. I have never been able to play retracements satisfactorily. They represent weakness in an upmove and my experience in the stock market has conditioned me to buy strength. So I do not try to buy the defining point below a reaction point in an upmove. I would far rather buy the take-out of the reaction point. But it is clear I make less money this way if that was what the market was going to do anyway. The only problem with retracements is that the market may just keep on retracing!

Experiment with **Staircase**. It offers a way of forcing yourself to join a strong move. So what if you miss 100 or even 200 points! When the S&P decides to go, it really goes. Just look at some of the charts in this manual and think of the potential profits out there. One can also toggle between an SP chart and a candlestick chart and use the second three-minute candlestick for entry. **Buy** the take-out of the high, **sell** the take-out of the low.

May 24, 1996

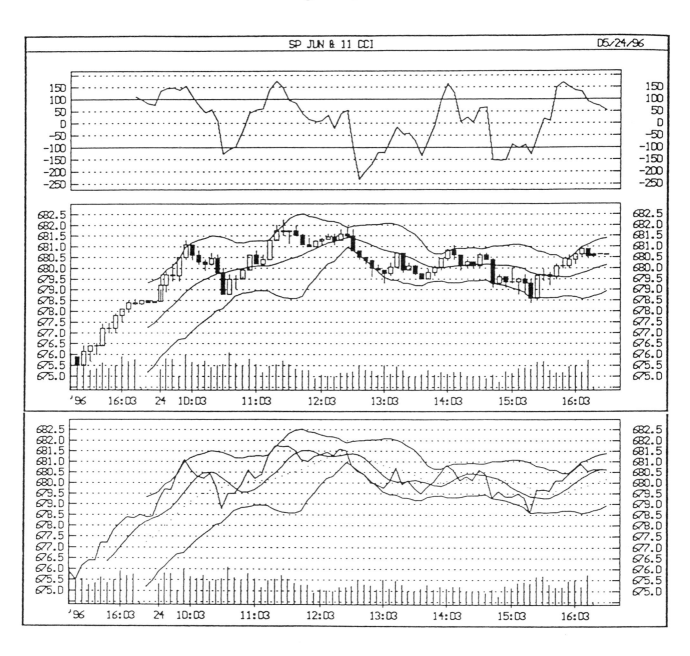

	679.20	682.25	678.40	680.65
			P/L	
Angler:	↑ 676.85	NT		
Embryo:	B 681.00	S 679.75	-1.25	
Ravine:	NT			

The Psychology of Trading

Let us return to the game of golf for a moment. Imagine a lone golfer on the last green facing a tricky 4-foot putt for an outright win. What Nick Faldo would call a "smelly little putt." If the golfer is an amateur, all that will be lost, if he misses, is the glory. The professional, if he misses, will receive a reduced paycheck. In each case the anguish, while very real, is not compounded by the extraction of a fine. Missing is punishment enough.

But in trading, the score is kept in dollars, and the trader is fined for making a bad trade. If enough bad trades are made, it is likely that trading will not continue for very long as there is a definite risk of ruin.

So it bears repeating that trading should only be done with 'funny money' — like Brazilian Cruzeiros before they were revalued. It should never be done with grocery money nor with college account money, only discretionary money.

A 50 point stop is tiny — almost certainly too small, and very easy for the floor traders to knock off. But it represents $250 of our hard-earned money, money which will buy some significant life pleasures. A bottle of *Dom Perignon* can be bought for about $100 and dinner for two in a first-class restaurant can usually be had for $250.

Personally, I hate to lose. I am sure everyone does, but my desire not to lose means I have difficulty letting the trade evolve naturally, so I tend to grab profits early to avoid a loss (the fine). This is known as leaving money on the table. Another problem I have had is that of "pulling the trigger." Trading from a live data feed is very difficult because of the inevitable randomness of the intraday action. So you wait to pick your spot; say you have decided you want to buy if the market corrects to a moving average value. What happens falls into one of three categories.

1. The market corrects to the MA value and you get a great fill. The only problem is that the market keeps on going in the wrong direction and every tick costs.

2. The market fails to correct. It shoots up on you, leaving you without a good place to climb aboard (**Staircase** will help).

3. Of course the market may do exactly what you expect — fall to the MA value, then take off on the upside. This is less likely than #1 or #2.

May 28, 1996

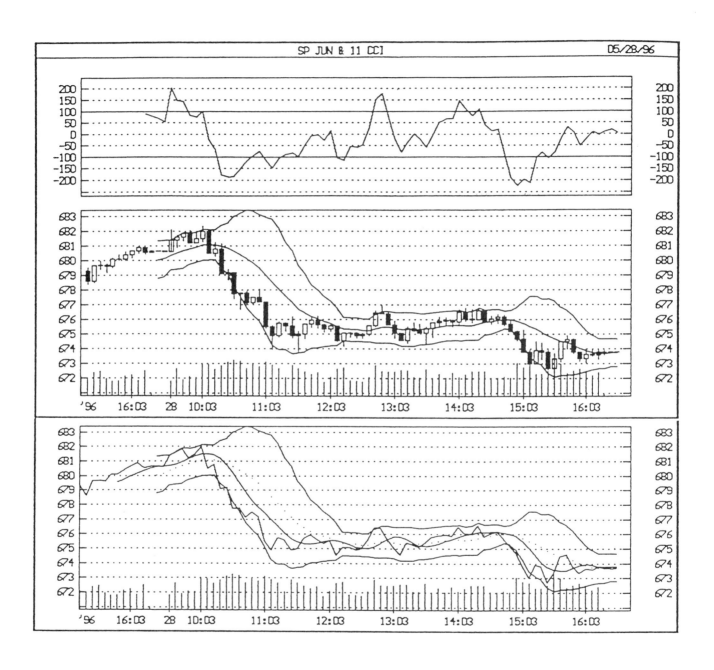

	682.10	682.35	671.90	673.80

P/L

Angler: ↑ 678.75   NT

Embryo: S 680.30   B 677.95   +2.35

Ravine: S 674.95   B 672.90   +2.05

Comment: 3 sell #3 signals (pg. 101). Market closed below its 0.3 EMA denoting a short term trend change.

Compounding the randomness of the intraday action is the multiplier of 500. I suspect many new-comers to trading are blown out of the water by a few big early losses.

Intraday trading demands much more skill than does overnight trading in stocks and mutual funds. If I am in a stock, I like to know during the day what it is doing. I like to know if my stops are threatened. But beyond that, what that stock does intraday is not much of a concern. I like it when it goes up---and I have to analyze it when it goes down. But I never look at it bobbing up and down during the day, the way I look at the S&P's.

There are many psychological problems associated with day trading — here's a partial list.

1. If trading from a computer screen, I have **to be there** and **be focused**.

2. This ties my day up significantly. Of course, if I view my trading as a business, this should not be a problem.

3. But it is boring and tiring much of the time, sitting in front of the screen waiting for something to happen.

4. So a quick trip to the post office is taken, or some other small errand.

5. *Caramba!* On my return 30 minutes later, not only has the market moved dramatically, but my stops may have been hit.

6. If I am going out, I may have put stop orders in with not-held contingency protective stops.

7. If the chairman of the Federal Reserve Board happens to speak to Congress or some unexpected fundamental event occurs, I may find that both my stops have been hit, handing me a ready-made loss.

8. So I avoid putting such orders in now and only trade when I can watch what is going on.

9. But the real problem is the trade itself. Once the trade is on and the protective stop is in, I am the captive of the trade and I find this an edgy feeling. I have not (yet) found a way of relaxing on the trade and just let it do its thing.

May 29, 1996

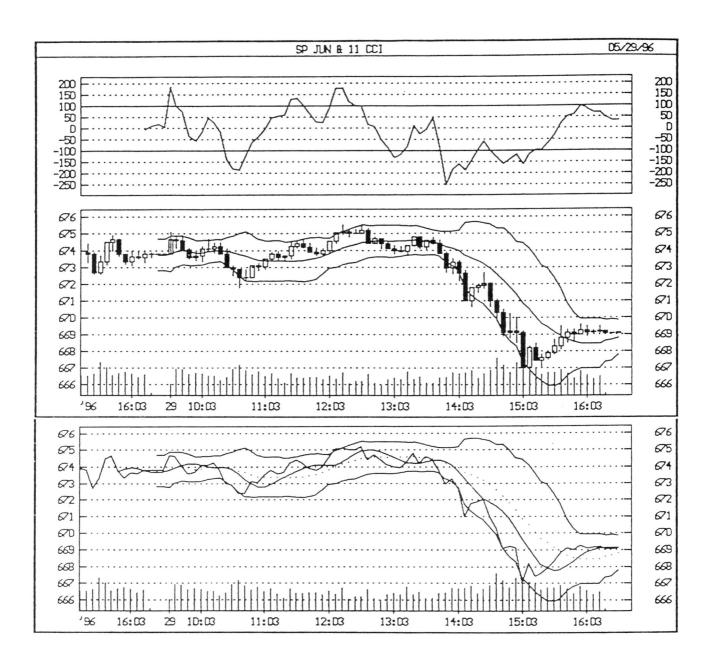

	674.60	675.50	666.30	669.10
			P/L	
Angler:	↓ 674.85	S 674.85	B 673.50	+1.35
Embryo:	S 672.80	B 671.55		+1.25
Ravine:	S 673.60	B 671.90		+1.70
Comment:	A lot left on the table by both **Angler** and **Embryo**.			

Larry Williams advises repetition as a way of desensitizing oneself to the stress. He went to Las Vegas and took hundreds of bets so he got used to getting the money down; also to winning and losing. He made the remark that while the movie *The Exorcist* was incredibly scary on first viewing, he knew that it would get progressively less scary on each subsequent viewing. The same approach works in futures trading if you give it a chance. I have the problem of wanting to be correct. I am discussing my own problems as I am sure they are not unique. As everyone knows, fear and greed are the foes and both have a bad effect on the bottom line. It is fear of a loss that drives me out of a trade prematurely. This surprises me as I am not a coward as the picture of me skydiving over the island of *Providenciales* (Provo) in the Turks and Caicos shows. Well, I still get uptight when trading and annoyed with myself when I miss an opportunity or make a stupid mistake. But I do notice that I am being less demanding of myself as I mature as a futures trader.

This manual is being written for David and other intelligent newcomers to the game. Interestingly, intelligence, as such, does not have a great deal to do with success. Success is elusive because nothing works all the time and great setups on one occasion can lead to unexpected losses on another.

All of which leads me to a very real question, "Is it worth all the trouble, expense, and aggravation to learn to trade futures properly?" The only answer is to try to find out I suppose, but if you ever manage to get good at it, man is it worth it.

It pays to have realistic goals when trading. No one gets good at anything without considerable effort and application. As the famous sculptor Michelangelo said, "If you knew how hard I had to work to achieve my mastery, it would not seem wonderful at all." So for the first year or two, a realistic goal would be to stay in the game with most of one's capital intact. I lost far more than was comfortable-if indeed losses are ever comfortable. I am giving myself to the end of the year to get good. I mean ego-satisfyingly good. It is important to feel that a significant level of competence has been achieved. I am not talking superstar status, just a steady golf 6 or 7 handicap performance, not a hacker nor, perish the thought, a shanker. Also, I will call it a day if my account equity falls to point X, the predetermined point at which I will get out immediately.

May 30, 1996

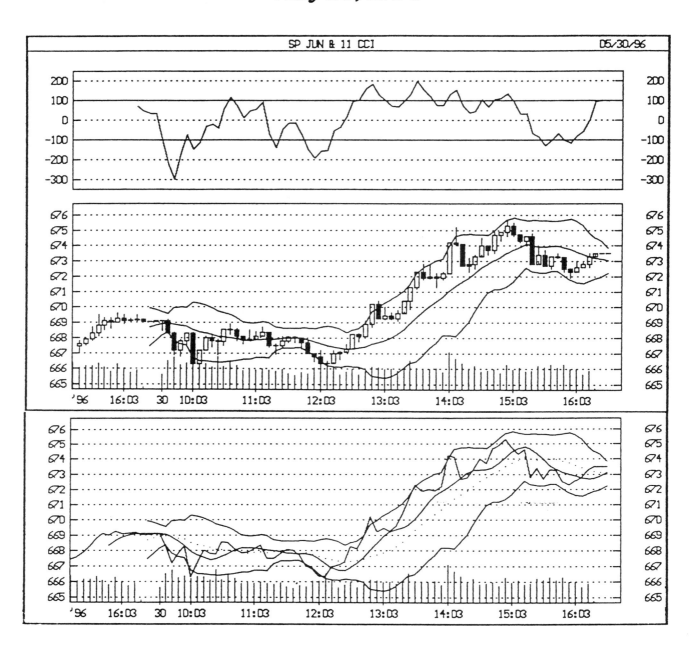

	668.45	675.70	665.70		673.40
			P/L		
Angler:	↓ 671.50	S 671.50	B 672.75	-1.25	
Embryo:	B 670.25	S 671.50		+1.25	
Ravine:	NT				

Comment: As the CCI crosses back from below +100 to above it, it gives good continuation buys when the market is running.

I mention this under psychological factors as it is important not to beat up on oneself. Not everyone was meant to be a trader. Give it a shot-if you can get it to work, fine; if not, move on. The reality of some traders persisting and persisting while driving themselves ever closer to ruin does not make any sense.

Traders are said to get what they deserve from the market — that somehow if you lose you secretly want to lose. I say "baloney" to that. In mutual fund trading from 10-8-82 to 4-3-84, I had a string of 15 winning trades without a single loss for a year and a half. I expect to win. I realize in the futures market I have to accept losses, but I just did not realize the number of ways in which I could lose and the kind of mistakes that lose money. Which is, of course, why I wrote this book.

Before we leave the psychology of trading, I should mention a mistake I have caught myself making. I call it blocking. Here is an example — I have a small successful morning trad I go out during the noon hour. When I return I fail, for one reason or another, to put on a trade that I would have taken in the morning. This trade, of course, turns out to be a corker. Blocking is caused by the fear of losing and can take many guises. Sometimes, if the telephone rings at just the wrong time or someone comes to the door, the blocking process has allies. However, the real problem is internal and has to be worked on if you identify it in yourself. But also be aware that it is easy to get too self-analytical. All that one should try to achieve — all that needs to be achieved — is to trade with a calm mind and sense of detachment, and to stop worrying about the money. "Scared money never wins."

OK, Let's Trade Futures

At this point order entry should not be a problem — the actual mechanism and type of order to use that is. But how should one go about trying to take some money from the market? I am going to assume that you will be trading from a live quote screen. As stated, I use *Signal* and MetaStock™. I have MetaStock™ set up in units of three minutes, so the next longer time frame is six minutes, then nine, etc. I find the six minute chart suits me well. There is little difference between six minute charts and the five minute charts often referred to in the literature.

So set up a 6-minute chart with thirteen bar moving average and associated Bollinger Bands. Now run a triangular MA 7 and an 11 bar CCI and you are in business.

May 29-30, 1996

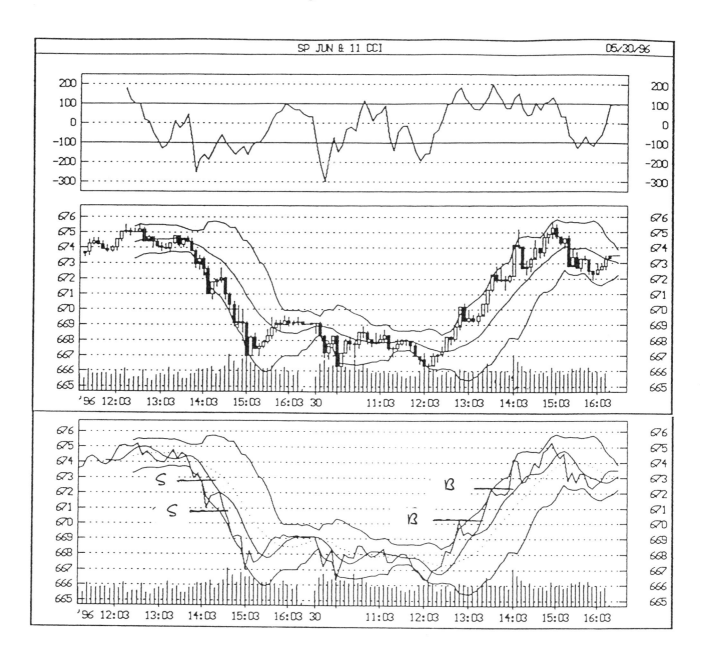

Sell signals #1 and
Buy signals #1 are about as clear as they come.

Sign of the Bear and **Sign the of Bull**

I am going to suggest just two buy signals and three sell signals. Further, I am going to suggest that you try trading just these signals on the buddy approach that I mentioned earlier before going live.

Buy Signals

Buy Signal #1

This signal we have already discussed. The market on the SP chart has to arrive at an upper Bollinger Band and that band has to turn up or already have turned up.

Ideally, the market should form a reaction point (RP) identified by a lower defining point (DP). Entry can then be made by one of the three methods described previously. (pg. 51)

But what happens if the move is really strong and no RP occurs? Here we have to toggle to a candlestick chart. The formation there is of two white candlesticks and entry is on the take out of the higher high of the **second** candle.

The protective stop should be the take-out, by one tick, of the low of the candle that got you to the Bollinger Band. **Try to stay in the trade as long as the market tracks above the TMA 7.**

The important thing to realize about buy signal #1 is that it is designed to enter the market **only** when and if the market tips its hand by acting strongly.

This signal has about a 65% chance of success. Note the CCI 11 will not be of much use as it will show the market is overbought. What we are hoping for is that the market gets more overbought.

Buy Signal #2

This signal is somewhat less reliable than buy signal #1, but it is a solid performer nonetheless. Here is the set up.

1. The market has to have reached the **lower** Bollinger Band. The CCI will have fallen below -100.

2. Now the market turns around and starts working its way higher.

3. The buy signal occurs around the TMA 7 line after the market has closed above that line and the CCI value rises above -100.

4. The ideal set-up is a small white candle whose real body is entirely above the TMA-7 line - on the chart it will look "cradled" by the line which will be turning up.

May 31, 1996

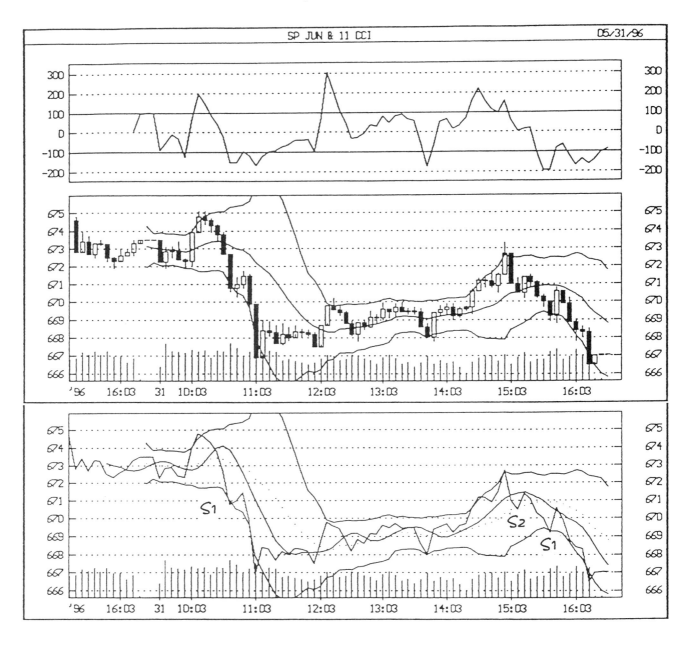

	672.60	**675.10**	**666.50**	**667.05**	
			P/L		
Angler:	↓ 673.60	S 673.60	B 671.55	+2.05	
Embryo:	B 674.40	S 673.15	- 1.25 }	+1.70	
	S 670.80	B 667.85	+2.95		
Ravine:	NT				
Comment:	**Angler** took some profit out of the short term trend. Note sell signals.				

5. The protective stop is below the TMA 7 line, one tick below the low of the candle that gave the signal.

6. Stay with the trade as long as the market keeps tracking **above** TMA 7.

These two signals are the only buy signals I suggest. I have experimented with a number of others. These two are the best I have found. Note in both cases the market has to reach a Bollinger Band for the set up to occur.

Sell Signals

Sell Signal #1

This is just the opposite of buy signal #1. The market has to reach the lower Bollinger Band. Market entry is on take-out of an RP, or if one fails to form, the lower low of the second successive black candle. The CCI 11 will not be useful.

The protective stop is the take-out of the high of the candle that got you there or a money man agement stop. Stay in the trade as long as the market tracks **below** TMA 7.

Sell Signal #2

This is just the opposite of buy signal #2. It occurs at the end of an up move. The market will have hit the **upper** band and then start falling away from it. The set up is a black candle whose real body is below---or mainly below---the TMA 7 line. The protective stop is a take out of the high of the black candle that got you there or a money management stop above the TMA 7 line.

Stay with the trade as long as it tracks **below** TMA 7.

Sell Signal #3

This signal is one that occurs during a quiet market time. The opposite buy setup is not as reliable and is not featured.

The set up:

1. Wait for the market to hit the upper Bollinger Band with a white candle.

2. The band will bulge a little as the candle hits it. **But then it has to stay flat.**

3. The CCI 11 is above +100.

4. The market now **fails to advance** and a black candle forms.

Feb 15, 1996

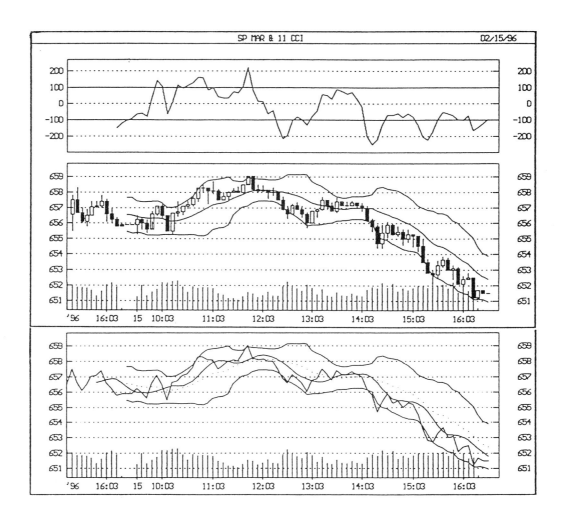

Sell Signal #3

Pure signal just before noon.

5. Sell the close of the black candle.

The protective stop is a take-out of the original white candle high. Stay with the trade until it reaches the lower Bollinger Band---then exit.

I hesitated to include this signal since I was not going to include the equivalent buy as that signal does not set up as well as the sell. This sell signal should be good for 100 points or so. As I say, it is received during a flat market period. If the market looks like it is in Ravine, be careful as the time in the Ravine expands. You want to avoid getting caught in an upside breakout that does not look back.

These five signals can, of course, be used on other time frames, but if you are watching the screen during the day, you will probably find yourself going with the shorter time frames. I have no experience of one minute bars, but even 3 minute bars are too fussy for my taste (except for **Staircase**). But all — and it takes time and diligence — the trader has to do is find an approach that works and then stick to it. Nothing works all the time and it is a mistake to switch from one approach to another just because the former was in a period of drawdown. Just as golfers go through periods of holing a high percentage of 6-foot putts to periods when they can't buy one, so do trading patterns go through periods of over---and under---performance.

But what if trading futures is too nerve-wracking? Is there a way to slow the action down without missing out on it entirely? Yes, indeed. *voila'*-it means look there — in our case, **options**.

OPTIONS: A SHORT COURSE

Option Terminology

An **option** is a contract between two individuals. The option **seller** writes the contract and defines its terms. These are: the strike or exercise price of the contract and the expiration month.

For a **call** option, the seller agrees with the **buyer** of that option to deliver a long futures contract to the buyer at any time the buyer decides to exercise this right. For this privilege, a premium is paid to the seller, the cost being decided between them by competitive bidding. If the Dec S&P futures contract is trading at 632, for example, the Dec 630 call will have 200 points ($2.00 [632.00 - 630.00]) of intrinsic value. It will be in-the-money. Let us say that 600 points ($6.00) was paid (cost to buyer $6 x 500 = $3,000). That's 200 points of intrinsic value plus 400 points of time premium with no value other than those points represent a position — a call on possible appreciation of the contract.

Feb 5 -21, 1996

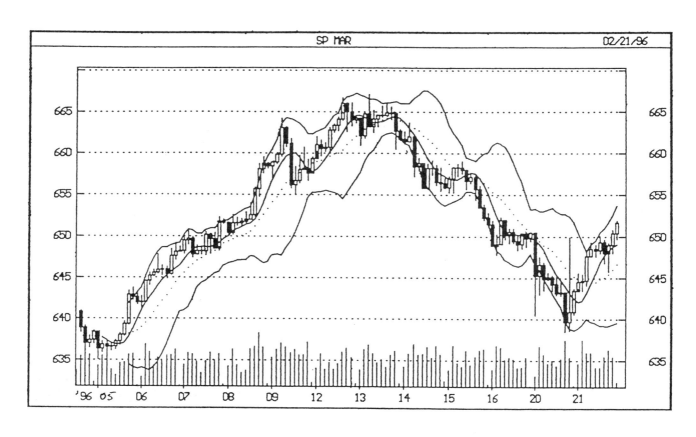

Option Country

Feb 5	BUY	Feb	645	CALL	-		3.60
Feb 12	SELL	Feb	645	CALL	-		19.95
Feb 13	BUY	Mar[x]	660	PUT	-		9.50
Feb 20	SELL	Mar	660	PUT	-		19.85

Profit before commissions and slippage CALL $8175
PUT $5175

[x] **Mar** because close to expiration of Feb series

WARNING: It is not as easy as it looks.

So the futures go to 640 and the option goes to 1200 ($12.00). What can the buyer do?

1. **The option can be exercised**. The buyer receives a long futures contract valued at 630. If it is sold immediately, the profit will be 640-630 less option cost of 600 points = 400 points profit ($4.00 x 500 = $2,000). For this example we will ignore commission costs.

2. The option bought can be sold **as an option**. This would yield a profit of 600 points (1200-600). That's $3,000.

It is clear that the option strategist is much better off selling the option bought at a **closing transaction** rather than exercising it, as the option still has some time value (200 points) over the intrinsic value of 1000 points. Of course, the buyer is in sole command of the action taken. The buyer does not have to sell the long option, nor exercise it.

On the other side of the contract, the seller can terminate the option sold by **buying** a similar option canceling the position. The seller of a call option may however be **assigned**---it occurs on a randomized basis---a short futures contract at any time. This is a real danger when the option traded consists of intrinsic value only. Once assigned, the short position has to be accepted and cannot be offset by the purchase of a matching option. The seller makes a profit when a similar option (in strike price and expiration month) can be purchased for less than the sale price. If the seller of a call option has no off-setting long futures position that can be delivered, that seller is **short a naked call option.** The seller's maximum profit will be achieved if the option expires worthless. The possible loss has no maximum. If the market goes up, up, up and away, the seller will be exposed to devastating losses. Evasive action may be taken by buying back the call sold (at a loss, of course) or converting the position into a **spread** by buying an option of different strike price. **This will lock in the loss**, but stop it running away. It is better just to buy back the option sold as soon as the position runs against the seller; better yet (see later) is to avoid selling naked options entirely.

So, an option with intrinsic value is *in-the-money*, one with no intrinsic value is *out-of-the-money* and one with strike price coincident with the present futures price is *at-the-money*. And a call option gives the buyer the right to acquire a long futures position at the option strike price. What about **puts**? Puts are the mirror image of calls. A put option gives the buyer the right to acquire a short futures position and the put option seller runs the risk of being assigned a long futures contract. Let's see how this might work in practice. We will use April 8 as a shining example of the risks and rewards involved. We will use the option prices quoted in *Investors Business Daily* and study both puts and calls.

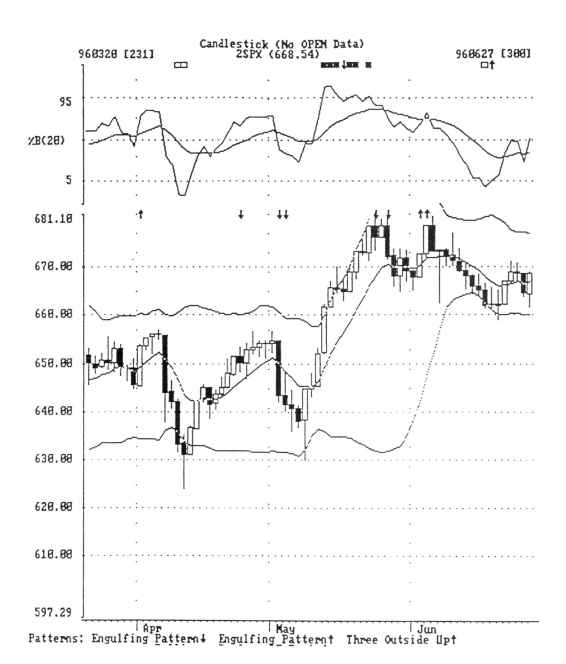

Overview of April and May 1996 Action

On Friday, April 4 the Jun S&P futures contract closed at 659.60. The in-the-money 655 April **call** closed at 10.15 (10.15 x 500 = a cost of $5,075). The out-of-the-money 600 April call closed at 7.00 ($3,500). Positions are taken on the close April 4.

We know what happened on April 8. There was a limit down opening gap of 1200 points. The market fell further only to recover to down 1260 points at 647.00 at the close of trading.

Here are the closing option prices on April 8:

> 655 call 3.00
> 660 call 1.60

The 655 call buyer lost $3,575 (10.15 - 3.00 x 500).

The 655 call seller made $3,575. Figures for the 600 call are $2,700 lost by the buyer, gained by the seller. And with **put** options the situation on the close of April 4 was as follows. The in-the-money 660 April put option closed at 7.40 ($3,700), the out-of-the-money 655 put at 5.55 ($2,775).

The prices at the close on April 8 were:

> 660 put 14.50
> 655 put 12.80

The buyer of the 660 April put option made 14.50-7.40 x 500 = $3,550 (96% in one day's trading). The seller lost a similar amount. For the 655 put the figure was $3,625; won by the buyer, lost by the seller. The market was not through with its downside action however. On April 10 the Jun contract closed at 633.25. Here are the option prices.

> 655 call 0.90   655 put 20.50
> 660 call 0.40   660 put 21.00

The winners are:
The 655 put buyers   + $7,475 (20.50 - 5.55. April 4 price)
and the 655 call sellers   + $4,625 (10.15 April 4 sale price - 0.90)

Note how the put buyers do and will always do better in a big down move than the call sellers as the maximum possible gain for the call sellers is the amount received, whereas the value of the long put will increase as long as the market keeps falling.

May 2-17, 1996

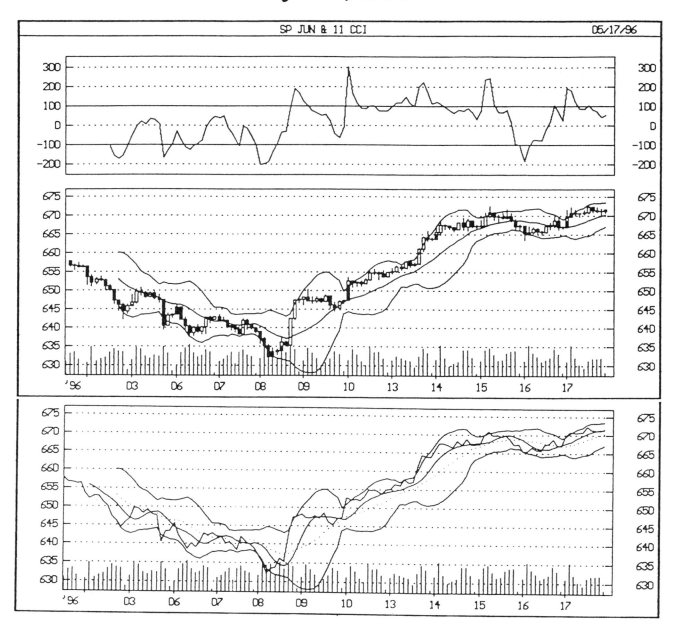

May Action #1   45 minute candles

There are some other option terms that need to be mentioned.

Premium: I usually avoid this term on its own as it is used by some traders to describe the total price of an option. I only use it with the qualifier-over intrinsic value-so there is no doubt that I am referring to pure premium-time value.

Delta: This is the amount that an option can be expected to move in relation to a move in the underlying instrument (futures, stocks or indices). As a rule of thumb, an at-the-money option is expected to move at about 50% of the rate of the underlying instrument.

If the futures move 200 points, the at-the-money option should move 100. It has a delta of 50.

Volatility: This term refers to the amount of movement and how quickly it occurs in the underlying futures contract. Historical volatility relates to a given time frame in the past and implied volatility (an important concept beyond the scope of this introduction to options) is the market's assessment of how volatile the action is going to be in the future. Fortunately, there is a visual aid that will supply you with all the information you need to have about volatility-John Bollinger's famous bands. When the bands contract and flatten out volatility is low-the market is in the ravine. A break out is coming. When volatility is high, the bands will balloon above and below the market drawing immediate attention to that fact.

Two other Greek terms, *vega*, the change in option price related to volatility and *theta*, the amount of value lost each day due to time decay.

Option strategies can get very complicated but for our purposes one should try, if buying an option, to do so at a period of low volatility when the option is likely to be fairly or even under-priced. And if setting up **spreads**, the parameters I will give will assure receiving enough from the option sold to justify the spread.

Option Strategies

These are the option strategies that I recommend presently:[20]

1. Straight purchase of puts or calls

2. Bullish put spread

3. Bearish call spread

We will consider each in turn.

May 16-31, 1996

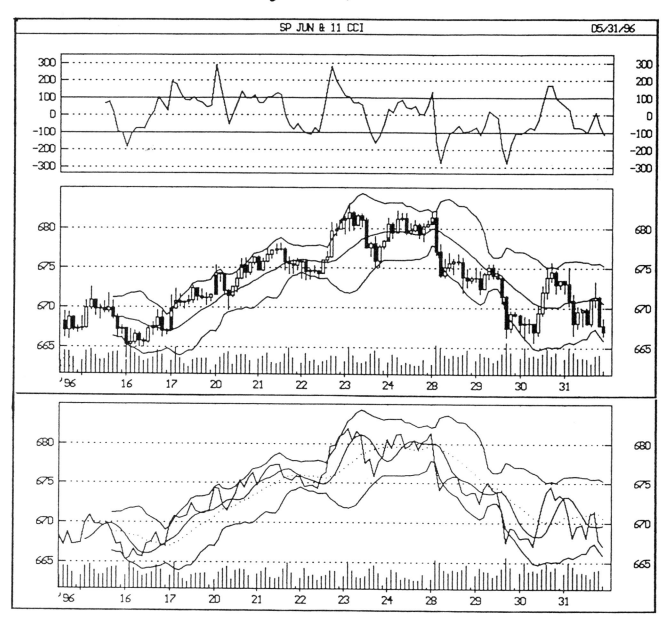

May Action #2   45 minute candles

1. Straight Purchase of Puts and Calls

This is the most straight forward option strategy. An at-the-money option can offer some significant advantages over a position in futures, namely,

a) the absolute loss is predetermined (but of course does not have to be taken).

b) moves against the position can be endured with an equanimity not available to the futures trader.

c) longer term position trades become possible without having to worry too much about large opening gaps — indeed I believe in position trading to go either with options or with mutual funds and to avoid overnight futures positions altogether.

So what are the disadvantages? Unfortunately, they are not inconsequential.

a) **The cost**: At 500 x the stated price a call option valued at 8.00 costs $4,000. Note it is always better to buy the most expensive option one can afford and to try for some intrinsic value or at least to be as close to the money as possible.

b) **The time decay factor**: this can be largely overcome by trading options short term. The time decay over 5-7 trading days is small.

c) **The volatility factor**: when the market begins to run option prices expand dramatically. This works as a distinct negative for the buyer of options if the move is well under way.

So, how should the straight purchase of puts and calls be traded? The rules are fairly straight forward.

a) You should monitor the underlying futures market from time to time during the day and adjust your option positions if necessary during the day. Do not expect to be very successful using the strategy of taking a position and holding it without monitoring it.

b) Trade off 30, 45 or 60 minute charts, but realize you are **trading** not **holding**.

c) Use Bollinger Bands and the buy and sell signals already described.

d) In purchasing options you can afford to be a bit early and anticipatory.

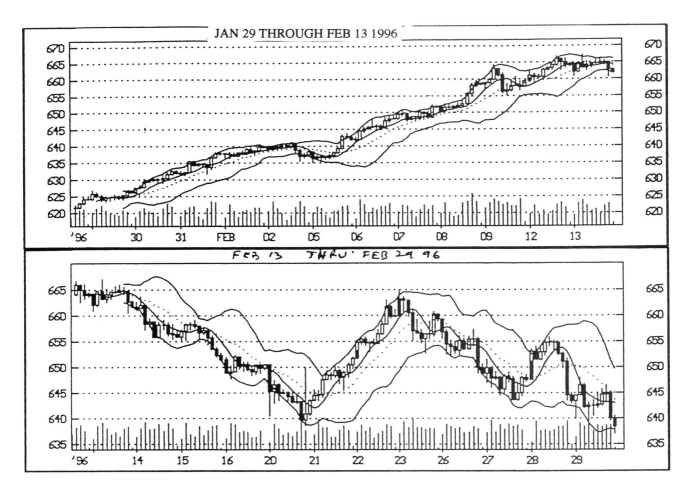

FEB 13 THRU FEB 29 96

The Analysis of a Free Trade
45 Minute Candle Chart

On January 30th (upper chart) a longer term investor might decide to buy an April 635 call for 13.65. On Feb 13 the market looked short term toppy, so an Apr 665 call is sold for 16.05 (more than was paid for the original long call---which closed at 39.80).

The market does indeed correct. The short 665 call is covered on Feb 21 as the Bollinger Bands and TMA 7 have turned up. (At 9.55 for a gain of 650 points). The 635 call closed on Feb 21 at 28.50 rising to 35.25 on Feb 22. The short call has provided protection---and some overall profit.

e) Do not risk more than 50% of your original purchase price.

f) Decide on the kind of market moves you wish to profit from and make sure that if the market moves, say 750 points, you either exit with a nice profit or sell an option, with strike price above the original strike price for calls, below it for puts for a sale price to you **greater than your original cost**. This is known as a **free trade**. What you have done is set up a riskless bullish spread with calls or a bearish spread with puts. If the market moves further in your favor, you will gain more on the original purchased option than you lose on the one sold. And if the market moves against you will be protected by the short side gain.

Conclusion

The straight purchase of puts and calls has repeatedly been branded as unsophisticated and naive. "Real" traders sell options (and get decapitated when the market opens limit down against their positions). If I have learned anything about trading options on futures, it is this (to be discussed in more detail at the end of this section) — do not sell unprotected "naked" options. This strategy may work 85-90% of the time, but if you are "naked," the other 10-15% of the time, the market will do you in.

I would like to draw your attention to the nearest thing I have found to low stress, not-watching-the-market option trading. This technique works very well in a volatile market when profits accrue to anyone on the right side of the market. It does **not** work very well in a trading range market unless you are prepared to "up" the supervision of the trade, and even then the results are definitely not as good as those obtainable in volatile trending markets.

The method is simple providing you have a program capable of "offsetting" (moving forward) a moving average. MetaStock™ has this capability. What we are going to be doing is run a 3-day triangular MA of the **lows** and a second 3-day TMA of the **lows** offset (moved forward) 2 days.

Jan-Jun, 1996

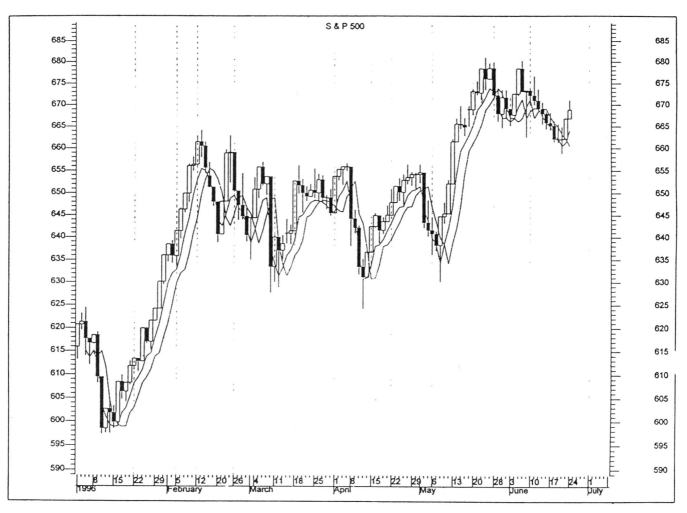

Chart Metastock™ 5.1 for Windows   S&P 500 Cash Index

The 3 Day MA of the lows with 2 Day Offset MA

Notice how clear the space between the two MA's is when the market is trending.
Note: Such charts are possible on MetaStock™ 4.52 RT, but not with this number of candles.

Here are the signals.

Buy: Buy the take-out---during the day---of the previous day's high providing that value is now **above** the 3 D. TMA offset 2. Give the set-up 3 ticks room.

Sell: Sell the take-out---during the day---of the previous day's low if it is now **below** the regular (not offset) 3 D. TMA of the **lows**. If you have a large opening gap that trades through your entry point, go back over the last 4 days to find a low to sell. Four days is as far back as you should go. This applies also to the buy side looking for a high to buy, but buy signals tend to spring up right out of the blue. May 8 is a perfect example. Be quick to turn bullish - slow to turn bearish.

Give sell signals 3 ticks as for buy signals. Both buy and sell option orders should be entered as **contingent orders**.

"Hi - This is Dave, A/C #12345. This is an option order good for today only. I wish to **buy**---that is buy---on a **contingent basis** 1 645 May S&P call if the market trades at 642.85." On May 8 the 645 may call closed at 5.15 ($2,575). It went off the board May 17 at 26.50 ($13,250) for a gain of $10,675.

2. **Bullish Put Spread**

3. **Bearish Call Spread**

These two spreads will be discussed together. Both these spreads are **credit** spreads — that is, more is received from the option sold than paid for the option bought.

To set up a **bullish spread sell** the higher strike (with calls or puts), **buy** the lower strike.

A bullish **put** spread receives more from sale of the higher strike put than is paid for the lower strike put. Obviously, the more that is received, the better. In credit spreads, the credit represents the possible profit. The difference between the strike prices and the credit received is the possible loss.

*So why set up a bullish spread with **puts** rather than **calls**? Here's why.*

1. You have an immediate credit. This is not of overriding importance but it provides a good feeling about the trade at its inception.

2. More importantly, if the market moves nicely in your favor and then starts looking like it is going to go the other way, you have the choice of covering the **short option** for profit leaving you with the long option.

April - June, 1996

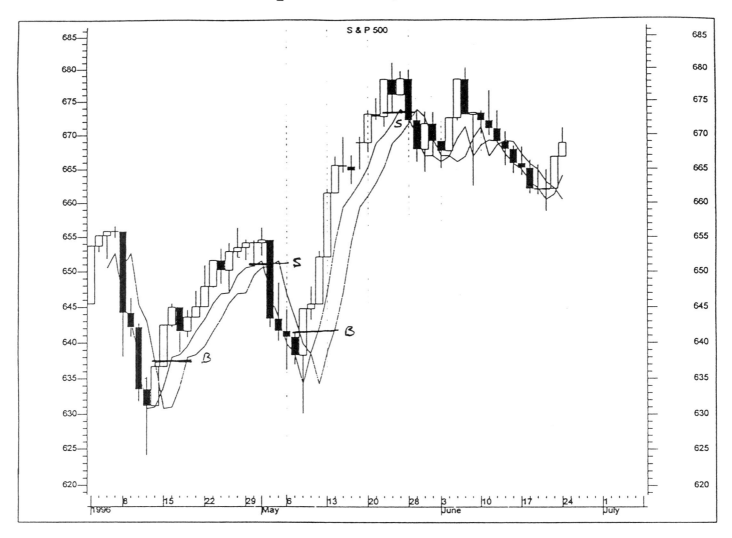

S&P 500 Cash Index

The 3 Day MA of the lows with 2 Day Offset

Closer View

3. If the spread had been made with calls, the winning option would be the **long** option. It is not a good idea to lift the long side of a spread leaving yourself with a naked short option.

The same reasoning applies to a **bearish spread** with calls.

To set up a bearish spread **buy** the higher strike (with calls or puts) **sell** the lower strike

A bearish **call** spread receives more from the sale of the lower strike call than is paid for the higher strike call. The problem with credit spreads is that it may be difficult to set them up with sufficient credit---the potential profit. It should be about **half the strike spread**---the difference between the strikes---seldom much less.

Options are difficult to trade well because of the number of variables. Here are some general suggestions.

1. When buying options, use the series next to expiration. Have a short term outlook - do not plan staying in the trade longer than a week unless the market is trending strongly in your favor.

2. Buy options in or at the money, certainly no further than one strike out.

3. Avoid the siren song of selling options.

4. Spreads need some time to work out. Time decay is not a major factor as it is gained by the short option in the spread. This balances the time decay of the long option.

Finally, in this section some advice about strangles. A **short strangle** consists of a short call option above the market and a short put option below it. The ideal scenario is a quiet trading range market with both options expiring worthless. It is like having your own money printing press; until, that is, the market gets volatile and starts running in one direction (as it did in much of 1995) or chopping violently (as in the early months of 1996). The problem when this happens is that the loss on the short option in the direction the market is moving is too big to be balanced by gain on the other option sold (which can only go to zero). The result is that losses mount quickly.

The first few strangles I put on worked like a charm and I believed I could protect the threatened short option by trading futures. For instance, a short strangle with a call or calls sold at a 640 strike and puts sold at a 600 strike would see the short calls threatened by a market rise close to 640. So why not **buy** a futures contract to protect this option? There are two serious problems with this approach.

SPH 95
Dec 94 - Feb 95

The Gap on February 3, 1995

1. One day, unexpectedly, the market may have a large upside opening gap which may not get filled, so **unless you were already long futures**, you have lost not only the amount of protection represented by the gap but also any additional amount before you got aboard. It happened to me on February 3, 1995 and it really hurt as I had 4 option contracts on each side of the strangle. This gap has still not been filled (written in May 1996).

2. The market may move around considerably during the period of few days so unless the move is sustained (and no one has a way of knowing if this will happen), the futures position may well end up showing a big loss **unless traded**, as the market settles back down and the 640 strike is no longer threatened. Please believe me on this one and avoid short strangles. I am referring only to short strangles using S&P options. David Kaplan is an expert in finding profitable short strangles in other futures contracts (bonds, currencies and hard commodities) and his book *Trade Like a Bookie* [21] gives the parameters to look out for.

I do not believe in holding positions overnight in the S&P futures market and I believe in only holding **long** positions or **spreads** overnight in the options market. So here is **Golden Rule #5**: *No overnight trades in the S&P except long options or spreads.*

Wrap Up

Well, at this point you will, I know, have developed an idea on which S&P course you are going to play. And it does not have to be just one. I have tried as concisely as possible to point out the pitfalls awaiting you and to suggest some trading patterns and strategies, but ultimately it all comes down to you as an individual. It is not enough to know how to trade, just as it is not enough to know how a golf ball should be hit. Each endeavor has to be undertaken. In golf it does not matter what your swing looks like or what gyrations you go through to produce it; what matters is---how does the ball behave? There is absolutely no doubt in the mind of anyone watching the shot, anyone who knows anything at all about golf that is, what kind of quality the shot has. If you drub it a few feet along the ground, obviously it has none. But you did make a swing at it and that is an important point.

May 31, 1996

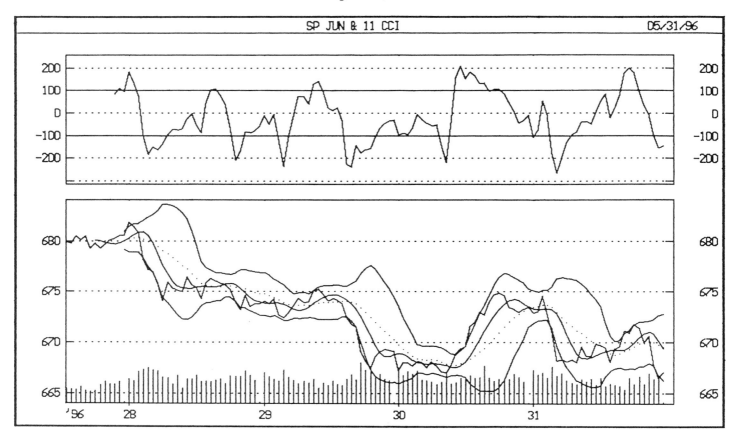

Preparing for Jun 3, 1996

Friday May 31 Readings

   672.60   675.10   666.50   667.05

Pivot #'s Mean $\dfrac{675.10 + 666.50 + 667.05}{3}$

= 669.55

Outer	**High**	**678.15**	1
Predicted	**High**	**672.60**	2
Predicted	**Low**	**664.00**	5
Outer	**Low**	**660.95**	6 (off the chart)
		TREND	
0.3 EMA (Friday Close)	**671.73**		3
Angler Bait Point	**669.40**		4

In the futures market a blow also has to be struck or the trigger has to be pulled or however you like to describe it. The reason I like using stops for entry is you can get the order down ahead of time, tee the ball up if you like. I am prepared to give up a few ticks, for the privilege of knowing that I will be aboard if I see the stop number hit on the screen. Playing the futures market is like playing one of those old "feathery" golf balls in a wind tunnel. The trouble is that the wind is variable and may blow the ball back in your face, causing you to believe you have missed the shot, only to have the wind change and gust your ball towards your target. And just as it is important in golf to go out to the practice range before a round to loosen up and work on one's timing, so is it important to prepare yourself for a trading session.

A trading suggestion: Before the trading session, print up a 15-minute chart of the contract you are trading, to include the last 3-5 trading days. Now mark off the previous significant high and low reversal points---use an SP chart. Work out the pivot numbers and mark them on the chart. Know what the daily trend has been and mark the **Angler** bait point and the closing 0.3 EMA values on the chart also. A good estimate of the daily trend as it applies to futures trading can be obtained from displays of regular and offset TMA 3 of the lows as we discussed under options. As soon as you know the opening price, mark the **Embryo** values on your chart also.

You may well notice that some values coincide. Pay special attention to these as support or resistance points. It is probably not a good idea to trade within the first 15-20 minutes of trading, but after that if a good RP forms, take it. The worst that can happen is that you are wrong early in the day with plenty of time left for the market to move your way. And if your first trade is successful, well, it certainly sets the day up nicely.

I suggest two trades a day---one in the morning session and one in the afternoon session. It is, of course, entirely a personal choice. I know one successful trader who flits in and out of the S&P all day, seldom winning or losing more than 50 points, but doing well. Ideally, one should stay in a trade until there is good evidence that the short term trend is reversed. This is where the triangular MA7 is a useful protective mechanism. I am afraid I cannot tell you how to stay in a trade any more specifically than that. If you trade with a profit objective, I suggest an MIT order rather than a limit order, as the latter may never get filled even if your price was hit briefly more than once. As we noted earlier, the market has to trade **through** your price for you to be sure of a fill on a limit order.

Feb 20, 1996

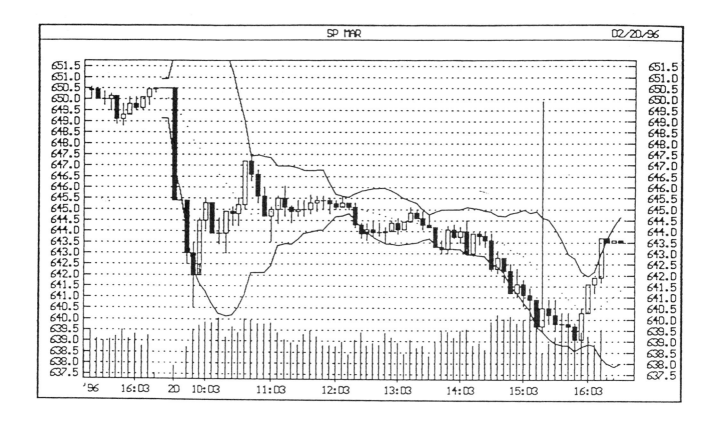

A Bad Number

Occasionally a really *'bad number'* occurs, which can cause all sorts of problems. Above is a really bad number late in the afternoon. Note also: when the chairman of the Federal Reserve Board addresses congress, you can expect some wild gyrations as bond traders try to interpret his statements. Such movements occur over the course of a few bars not, as above, in a single bar.

I have enjoyed writing this manual and know I am a better trader now than before I started it. Not great, but more patient and selective and definitely more detached. Writing has reminded me of the importance of detachment — the feeling of watching yourself trade and accepting wins and losses with equanimity. If you watch the S&P screen much during the day, you will quickly realize the large random element in the really short term ups and downs of the market. So, on any individual trade, the result will be random to a significant extent and will not be predictable with anything approaching finite accuracy. So I try to think in terms of a series of trades. I find three to be a good number. If I win all three trades in any set of three, I feel I am on the right track. If I lose all three trades, I know I am not and will stop trading for a short while. I like 2 wins, 1 loss, and accept 1 win, 2 losses, providing I don't keep doing that. At the end of 12 trades - 4 sets of 3 trades - I expect to win at least 7 or 8. More importantly, I must make sure to keep my losses no greater and hopefully smaller than my wins. Trading is a difficult game. No one expects to get good at a difficult game like golf without a considerable amount of practice. Why should trading be any different?

As a way of saying good-bye and wishing you well, I will leave you with some random thoughts and observations gleaned from re-reading my diaries. They are in no particular order.

1. It is essential for me to know what I will do if the market proves me 100% wrong.

2. Stop and reverse should usually be two operations.

3. If an unexpected market event occurs in my favor, I will accept it gratefully. There are other events less favorable by far, waiting in the wings.

4. Most opening gaps get filled during trading on the day of the gap. Only very rarely will a daily gap not get filled.

5. Gaps can be ignored by the day-trader, but to do so may overlook a trading opportunity.

6. Look to go counter to any sharp move but don't be in a hurry to do so.

7. You have to trade when the market is moving. This may well not coincide with the time you decide you want to trade it.

8. Allocate some "funny" money and play the market like a video game.

9. Test thoroughly before trading.

10. Try very hard to get aboard those big days. This is what **Embryo** is all about.

11. Never hold an opinion on what the market "should" do, especially what it should do in the next half hour.

Feb 9, 1996

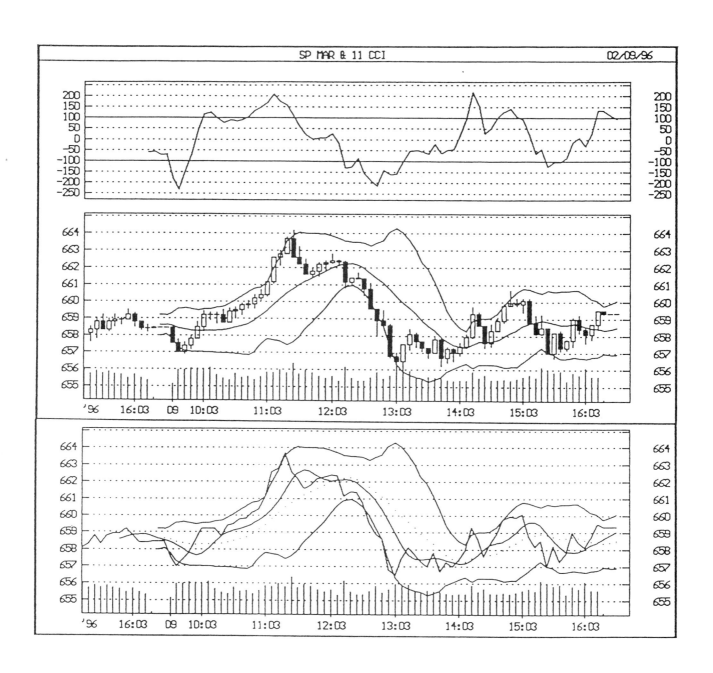

The Band of Five

Here is a formation -- not mentioned in the text -- that I would like to draw to your attention. It consists of five candles (on any time frame) with a long white candle followed by two small white candles then two black candles, the second of which gets back into the real body of the original white candle. <u>Sell</u> close of second black candle (11:15 AM).

13. Don't try to get even at all costs. Each trade has to be treated on its own merits.

14. Never "force" a trade. If it does not line up well, let it pass.

15. A consistent approach has the best chance of success.

16. Jump the gun. Have a tight stop and stop looking for a sure thing.

17. Don't trade when tired or depressed.

18. Don't wait around for a lot of confirming action. The train leaves promptly.

19. It is difficult to be too quick or too decisive.

20. Life and trading are to be enjoyed, not agonized over.

And, finally, a quotation I think I invented, I say 'I think' because I have had it as part of my philosophy for a long time now, and as far as I know, I never read it anywhere.

21. Nothing worth having is lightly won.

Here are some of my expensive mistakes.

1. Trading short strangles

2. Having too small stops

3. Having too large stops

4. Taking "iffy" trades

5. Exiting too quickly

6. Not exiting quickly enough

7. Trading too many contracts — one is fine to start.

Jan 29 - Feb 9 1996

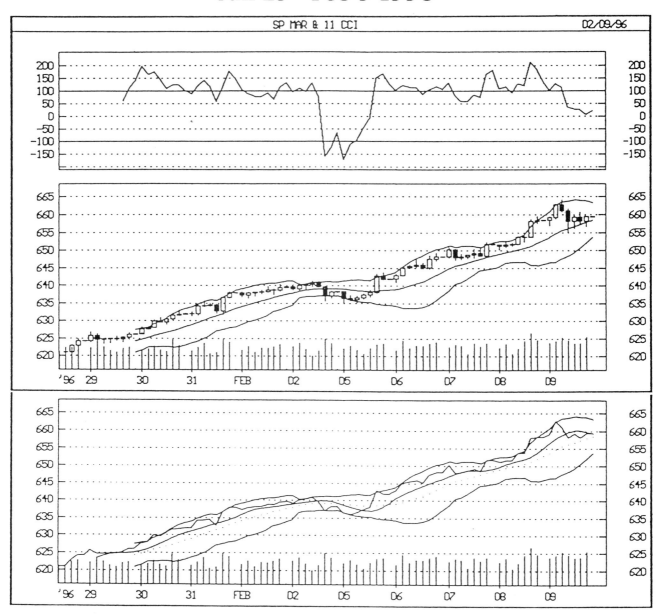

A Running Period

This is the final chart. I printed it up for you to compare with pg. 64 a pure running day on a six minute chart. A very similar formation takes place above on a 45 minute candle chart over 10 trading days. Notice the great W buy on CCI.

And here---collected---are

The Golden Rules

1. Use a protective stop on all futures trades.

2. Never give back all the potential profit.

3. Keep a trading diary.

4. Never take an indicator signal counter to a strongly trending market.

5. No overnight trades in the S&P except long options or spreads.

Five Final Trading Suggestions

1.   If you have trouble pulling the trigger, use the
JUMP-MASTER CHECKLIST
Time_____   Next_____   Min. Bar Closes At_____
When the Bar Closes (or is about to) ask yourself:
(1) Is the market at a Bollinger Band?_____
(2) Has the Band turned or appears about to?_____
    If **Yes** to 1 & 2, you have a **buy/sell alert.**
(3) Has the market started to run?_____
    Staircase Alert/Entry Signal
(4) Has an RP formed?_____
    If **Yes, pick up the phone and put an entry stop in.**

2. MetaStock™ has programming and system testing capabilities. But you will need accurate tick data to test your ideas. If you want extensive back testing to be done, I suggest you contact Futures Truth. John Hill, the owner, publishes a bimonthly review of all the trading systems in the public domain. In addition, a programming and system testing service is offered. George Pruitt is the head programmer. Futures Truth Co., 815 Hillside Road, Hendersonville, NC 28791 (704)696-2504. Bill Brower,[4] another excellent programmer, offers a similar service.

3. If you get a really bad fill, ask for a 'Time and Sales' check. Bad fills occur in a fast market and there is not much you can do about them, unless they are consistently bad, in which case you should change brokers.

4. When you get good, try trading 2 contracts. Pull one after a small profit, say of 50 points; let the other run with an initial break-even protective stop.

5. If you like the signals I describe but do not want to sit in front of the screen all day, I can give you the name of a very competent broker who will trade the signals you select for you. Drop me a line care of the publisher.

I hope I have been of help. May the trading gods smile on you.

ORDER FORM

TRADING ORDER FORM						
DATE			**DAY**			
A-C#			**Tel #**			
BUY						
SELL						
# MONTH						
STOP AT						
LIMIT OB						
ATM						
MIT						
TICKET #						
AGENT						
TIME						
CANCEL						
C/REPLACE						
TICKET #						
TIME						

The Jun S&P contract is **SPM.**

Note: Since Jun is the next contract to expire, your broker will assume you wish to trade this contract if you do not mention the month.

OPTION SPREAD ORDER FORM

DATE _____   DAY_____

AC#_____   TEL # 1-800_____

This is an S&P option spread order

TO OPEN_____   DAY ORDER_____
TO CLOSE_____   OPEN ORDER_____

I wish to
      BUY   SELL

#_____   #_____
MONTH_____   MONTH_____
STRIKE_____   STRIKE_____
TYPE_____   TYPE_____

    For a premium of _____OB

    To the_____

TICKET #_____
AGENT_____
TIME_____

Bibliography

1. Lloyd, Humphrey E.D. *The RSL Market Timing System*. Available through Traders Press, Inc., P.O. Box 6206, Greenville, SC 29606. 1990.

2. Lefevre, Edwin. *Reminiscences of a Stock Operator*. Available through Traders Press, Inc., P.O. Box 6206, Greenville, SC 29606

3. Kelly, Vilar F. 11 Pinecrest Drive, Flatrock, NC 28731 704-697-6502.

4. Brower, William B. *Inside Edge Systems*. 10 Fresenius Road, Westport, CT 06880. 203-454-2754.

5. Smith, Gary. *Live the Dream by Profitably Day Trading Stock Futures.*Available through Traders Press, Inc., P.O. Box 6206, Greenville, SC 29606. 1995.

6. *Signal*: Supplied by Data Broadcasting Corp., P. O. Box 8089, Foster City, CA 94404.

7. *MetaStock*™ Equis International Inc., 3950 South 700 East, Suite 100, Salt Lake City, UT 84107.

8. Williams, Larry. *Batting .800 The Money Tree: The Williams Way To Wealth*. British American, 18 Crow Canyon Court, Suite 200, San Ramon, CA 94583. 1995.

9. *Club 3000 News*™ Bo Thunman, Editor. 4563 North 38th Street, Augusta, MI 49012. 616-731-5600

10. Nison, Steve. *Japanese Candlestick Charting Techniques*. New York Institute of Finance, Simon and Schuster, NY. 1991.

11. Dobson, Edward D. *Understanding Bollinger Bands*. Traders Press, P. O. Box 6206, Greenville, SC 29606. 1994.

12. Ross, Joe. *Trading by the Minute.*Available through Traders Press, Inc., P.O. Box 6206, Greenville, SC 29606. 1991.

13. *MetaStock*™ *Users Manual Version 4.5* 1994, 3950 South 700 East, Suite 100, Salt Lake City, UT 84107.

14. Appel, Gerald. *Systems and Forecasts*, Signalert Corporation, 150 Great Neck Road, Great Neck, NY 11021.

15. Hulbert, Mark. *The Hulbert Financial Digest*, 316 Commerce Street, Alexandria, VA 22314.

16. Wilder, J. Welles, Jr. *New Concepts In Technical Trading Systems*.
Available through Traders Press, Inc., P.O. Box 6206, Greenville, SC 29606. 1978.

17. *Chicago Mercantile Exchange: Price Limit Guide*. This free guide explains the various rules governing limit moves and should be consulted. CME, 30 South Walker Drive, Chicago, IL 60606; 312-930-8233. 1995.

18. Moore, Ed and Conway, Joe, Ph.D. *Rhythm of the Markets*. 11 C Riverview Circle, North Bergen, NJ 07047. 1994.

19. Bernstein, Jake. *The Investors Quotient.*Available through Traders Press, Inc., P.O. Box 6206, Greenville, SC 29606. 1993.

20. Lloyd, Humphrey E.D. *High-Profit/Low Risk Option Strategies*. Windsor Books, P. O. Box 280, Brightwaters, NY 11918. 1984.

21. Caplan, David L. *Trade Like a Bookie*. Opportunities in Options, P. O. Box 5406, Oxnard, CA 93031. 1995.